MEDITERRANEAN PESCATARIAN COOKBOOK

2 Books In 1: Learn How
Cook At Home 140 Fish
Seafood And European
Recipes

Maki Blanc

MEDITERRANEAN
COOKBOOK

70 Recipes for Easy and Healthy Italian Greek Spanish and French Traditional Dishes

Maki Blanc

The trademarks that are used are without any consent, and the publication of the trademark is without permission or backing by the trademark owner. All trademarks and brands within this book are for clarifying purposes only and are the owned by the owners themselves, not affiliated with this document.

Contents

CHAPTER 3: THE WORLD OF PESCATARIAN DINNER RECIPES

CHAPTER 4: THE WORLD OF PESCATARIAN SNACK RECIPES 190

Introduction

Most people enjoy Mediterranean cuisine because it is among the healthiest on the planet. Since Mediterranean dishes are made from fresh ingredients, these recipes' positive effects make them even more delicious. New whole foods such as berries, grains, herbs, vegetables, and nuts are emphasized in the diet. Mediterranean food is a term that refers to food patterns that are followed by a diverse range of individuals. It is not the result of a single ethnic group or community. Cooking reflects a wide range of cultural influences.

The Mediterranean Sea was home to the world's first civilizations. The good soil and mild climate boosted food land. Their position at the crossroads of Europe, Asia, and Africa attracted merchants who traded cultural products such as seasoning and other foodstuffs. Another aspect that influenced Mediterranean delicacies was colonization. As a result of various societies' attempts to establish empires, the diverse cultures of the Mediterranean came under increasing contact.

Olive oil is one of the most widely used ingredients in Mediterranean cuisine. Olive trees can be found in abundance in the area. Olives are a key food in many dishes. Veggies are also a must-have. Common vegetables include zucchini, green beans, carrots, tomatoes, nuts and seeds, mushrooms, garlic, okra, eggplants, and a broad range of greens and courgettes. Food is seldom eaten. The rugged terrain of the Mediterranean does not sustain larger herding livestock like cattle, so goats, pigs, and poultry provide the bulk of the meat. Normally, it is roasted. Milk from goats and sheep can also be used in a number of recipes.

Seafood is readily available due to the city's proximity to the Mediterranean Sea. Mediterranean food is distinguished by the use of fresh herbs such as garlic, marjoram, tarragon, thyme, oregano, shallots, parsley, basil, and cloves. "Mediterranean Cookbook" is rich in tasty and delicious recipes from Mediterranean cuisine. It has four chapters. The first chapter is about traditional Italian cuisine. While Chapters two, three, and four are about Spanish, French, and Greek recipes. Start reading this book and enjoy Mediterranean food with more health benefits.

Chapter 1: Traditional Italian Dishes

1.1 Italian Oven Roasted Vegetables

Cooking Time: 30 minutes
Serving Size: 6

Ingredients:
- Parmesan cheese
- Crushed red pepper
- 1 teaspoon dried thyme
- Salt and pepper
- 8 oz. baby Bella mushrooms
- Extra virgin olive oil
- ½ tablespoon dried oregano
- 12 oz. baby potatoes
- 2 zucchini or summer squash
- 12 large garlic cloves
- 12 oz. Campari tomatoes

Method:
1. Preheat the oven to 375 degrees Fahrenheit.
2. In a big mixing bowl, combine the mushrooms, vegetables, and garlic.
3. Drizzle a generous amount of olive oil on top.
4. Insert the sesame oil, tarragon, salt, and pepper to taste. Toss all together.
5. Take just the potatoes and lay them out on a baking pan that has been lightly greased.
6. Roast for ten minutes in a preheated oven.
7. Remove the pan from the heat and add half veggies and mushrooms.
8. Return to the oven for a final 20 minutes of roasting or until the vegetables are fork-tender.
9. Mix thoroughly with smashed cayenne pepper and chopped fresh Parmesan cheese.

1.2 Mediterranean Pasta

Cooking Time: 20 minutes
Serving Size: 6
Ingredients:
- ¼ cup Parmesan cheese
- ¼ cup Italian parsley
- ¼-½ teaspoon red pepper flakes
- ¼ cup lemon juice
- 3 tablespoons olive oil
- ½ teaspoon black pepper
- 1 can artichoke hearts
- 1 can of black olives
- 1 tablespoon kosher salt
- 4 cloves garlic
- 2 cups grape tomatoes
- 6 ounces whole-wheat pasta

Method:
1. Bring 1 tablespoon salt to boiling in a big pot of water.
2. Add the noodles until it is al dente (firm to the bite).
3. Garlic should be minced; cherry tomatoes should be halved; artichokes should be drained and finely chopped; olives should be drained and sliced in half.
4. In a medium saucepan, heat the olive oil over moderate flame.
5. Combine the tomatoes, cloves, residual salt, pepper, and ground chili flakes in a large mixing bowl.
6. Cook, stirring regularly until the seasoning is fragrant and the tomatoes have broken down.
7. Toss the spaghetti in the skillet to coat it.
8. Combine the artichokes and olives in a bowl.

9. Pour the lime juice over the pasta and toss to combine.
10. Toss for another 2 minutes, or until heated through.
11. Remove from the heat and top with Parmesan cheese and tarragon.

1.3 Mediterranean Pasta Salad

Cooking Time: 15 minutes
Serving Size: 8

Ingredients:
Mediterranean Pasta Salad

- 4 ounces feta cheese
- Red onion
- 1-pint cherry tomatoes
- 2/3 cup Kalamata olives
- 1 English cucumber
- 12 ounces dry pasta

Lemon-Herb Vinaigrette

- ¼ teaspoon salt
- Pinch of red pepper flakes
- 2 small garlic cloves
- ¼ teaspoon black pepper
- ¼ cup olive oil
- 2 teaspoons dried oregano
- 1 teaspoon honey
- 1 tablespoon lemon juice
- 3 tablespoons red wine vinegar

Method:

1. Cook the noodles al dente as per package directions in a big soup pot of simmering water.
2. Drain pasta and rinse for 20-30 seconds underneath cold water until it is no longer wet.
3. In a large bowl, position the pasta.

4. Toss together the tomatoes, cucumber, feta cheese, Kalamata olives, and red onion in a stand mixer, then sprinkle the vinaigrette over all evenly.
5. Toss till the dressing is uniformly distributed between the components.
6. Serve right away, with extra feta and black pepper on top if needed.
7. Add all ingredients to a mixing bowl and whisk until smooth.

1.4 Simple Pancetta Pasta with Peas and Parmesan

Cooking Time: 23 minutes
Serving Size: 4
Ingredients:
- Salt and black pepper
- ½ lemon
- 2 cloves garlic
- ¼ cup Parmesan
- 16 ounces fettuccine
- ½ onion
- 1 (10-ounce) bag frozen peas
- 8 ounces pancetta

Method:
1. Over moderate flame, bring a big pot of salted water on the stove.
2. Cook until the pasta is al dente.
3. Drain the pasta, reserving 1 cup of the cooking liquid.
4. In a wide pan over medium heat, cook pancetta once golden brown, around 6 minutes. Place on a plate lined with paper towels.

5. Sauté onions in the very same pan until melted, around five minutes. Sauté the peas and cloves for three minutes.
6. Combine the Parmesan, pasta, and pancetta in a mixing bowl.
7. Use some of the stored pasta water to moisten the noodles.
8. Toss to mix, sprinkle with salt if desired, and top with lime juice drizzled on top.

1.5 Crispy Fried Calamari Recipe

Cooking Time: 50 minutes
Serving Size: 4
Ingredients:
- 2 tablespoons parmesan
- Black pepper
- Salt
- 1 tablespoon unsalted butter
- 2 tablespoons garlic olive oil
- 250 grams orzo pasta
- 625 milliliters boiling water
- 150 grams petits pois
- 150 grams pancetta

Method:
1. In a heavy-bottomed pan, heat the oil.
2. Heat, occasionally stirring, till the pancetta is crispy and freckled, then add the beans and mix for a minute or so, till the frozen look has disappeared.
3. Put in hot water after tossing the pasta in the pancetta and beans.
4. Add the salt, then reduce the heat to low and allow to simmer for ten minutes, checking on it a few times and stirring it or two to keep it from settling.

5. The water must be consumed by the pasta, which should be fluffy and starchy.
6. In a large mixing bowl, combine the butter and Parmesan, season with salt and pepper, and serve with rice into warm ready bowls.

1.6 White Bean and Kale Soup with Chicken

Cooking Time: 30 minutes
Serving Size: 6
Ingredients:
- Sea salt + black pepper
- 3 cups kale
- 1 15-oz can white beans
- 2 cups chicken
- 1 strip bacon
- 4 cloves garlic
- 8 cups broth
- 1 cup white onion
- 1 tablespoon avocado oil

Method:
1. Over moderate flame, heat a large pan or casserole dish.
2. Once the pan is warmed, add the bacon or oil.
3. Allow for two minutes of cooking time, stirring occasionally.
4. Cook, stirring periodically, for 4-5 minutes, or until onions becomes transparent and citrusy.
5. Then add garlic and cook for another 2-3 minutes.
6. Carry to a boil the broth, completely soaked white beans and meat.
7. To blend the flavors, cook for ten minutes.
8. After that, sprinkle with salt and pepper.
9. Insert the kale over the last few minutes before serving. Serve instantly.

1.7 Italian Baked Chicken Breast Recipe

Cooking Time: 30 minutes
Serving Size: 4

Ingredients:

- ¾ cup bread crumbs
- 4 chicken breast halves
- ½ cup Parmesan cheese
- ¾ teaspoon garlic powder
- ¾ cup mayonnaise

Method:

1. Preheat the oven to 425 degrees Fahrenheit.
2. Combine the mayo, Grated parmesan, and fresh basil in a mixing bowl.
3. Bread crumbs should be dropped in a different dish.
4. To cover the meat, dip it in the mayonnaise combination and then into the bread crumbs.
5. Arrange the poultry on a baking sheet that has been sprayed.
6. In a roasting tin, bake for 20 minutes or until meat juices run transparent and the surface is lightly browned.

1.8 Baked Zucchini with Parmesan and Thyme

Cooking Time: 30 minutes
Serving Size: 4

Ingredients:
- 2 tablespoons olive oil
- 2 tablespoon parsley leaves
- ¼ teaspoon garlic powder
- Kosher salt and black pepper
- 4 zucchini
- ½ teaspoon oregano
- ½ teaspoon basil
- ½ teaspoon thyme
- ½ cup Parmesan

Method:
1. Preheat the oven to 350 degrees Fahrenheit.
2. Set aside a broiler pan that has been sprayed with nonstick cooking spray and placed on a baking sheet.
3. Mix Parmesan, tarragon, marjoram, basil, garlic salt, seasoning, and pepper in a small cup, to fit.
4. Place the zucchini on the baking sheet that has been prepared.
5. Drizzle olive oil over the top and top with the Parmesan combination.
6. Preheat oven to 350°F and bake until vegetables are tender about thirty minutes.
7. Then reheat for 2-3 minutes, or until lightly browned and crispy.
8. Mix thoroughly with parsley on top, if desired.

1.9 Italian-Style Sheet Pan Chicken with Vegetables

Cooking Time: 40 minutes
Serving Size: 4

Ingredients:

- ¼ cup balsamic vinegar
- Fresh basil rolled
- 4 slices mozzarella cheese
- 2 tomatoes sliced
- Kosher salt to taste
- Black pepper to taste
- 4 chicken breasts
- ¾ cup marinade
- 3 cups broccoli florets
- 2 tablespoons olive oil
- 4 red potatoes

For the Marinade

- 1 teaspoon sugar
- 1 teaspoon red pepper flakes
- ½ tablespoon kosher salt
- 1 teaspoon black pepper
- 1 cup olive oil
- 1 tablespoon thyme
- 1 tablespoon basil
- 5 cloves garlic minced
- 1 tablespoon oregano
- 1 cup red wine vinegar

Method:

1. Combine all of the marinade ingredients in a mixing bowl and whisk until smooth.
2. Place the chicken in a plastic container with ¾ cup of the marinade and put the lid.
3. Set aside the remainder of the marinade.

4. Remove any excess air from the bag, close it tightly, and marinate for at least a few minutes.
5. Preheat the oven to 475 degrees Fahrenheit.
6. Toss the leftover marinade with the diced potatoes.
7. Arrange the potatoes in a single layer down one side of the plate.
8. Bake for 20 minutes in the oven.
9. Remove the pan from the oven after the chicken and vegetables have cooked for about twenty minutes and add the vegetables.
10.   Over the vegetables, sprinkle about 2 tablespoons olive oil and season with salt and pepper.
11.   Return the pan to the oven for fifteen minutes after coating the chicken with fresh mozzarella and tomato.

1.10 Eggplant Pizza Recipe with Spinach and Mushrooms

Cooking Time: 20 minutes
Serving Size: 6
Ingredients:
- 1 cup marinara sauce
- 10 oz. fresh mozzarella
- 6 ounces white mushrooms
- 2 cups baby spinach
- 1 eggplant
- Extra virgin olive oil
- Kosher salt

Method:
1. Preheat oven to 425 degrees Fahrenheit.
2. On both ends, sprinkle the eggplant with sea salt.
3. Rub an overly big baking sheet with olive oil.

4. Organize the eggplant slices in a thin layer on a baking sheet.
5. Cook for 20 to 30 minutes on the wire shelf of your preheated oven.
6. In the meantime, heat 1 tablespoon of additional vegetable oil in a pan.
7. Cook the mushroom for about five minutes over moderate flame.
8. Mix in the spinach for a few seconds to wilt it.
9. Return the baking sheet to the stove and set the oven to fry up.
10. Take the eggplant out of the oven and set it aside.
11. Overlay the eggplant slices with the mushrooms and spinach combination.

1.11 Chicken Stew Recipe, Mediterranean-Style

Cooking Time: 45 minutes
Serving Size: 6
Ingredients:
- 1 tablespoon white wine vinegar
- 1 cup fresh parsley
- 1 28 can tomatoes
- 2 cups chicken broth
- 1 teaspoon dry oregano
- 2 sprigs of fresh thyme
- 1½ lb. chicken thighs
- 1 teaspoon paprika
- 1 teaspoon coriander
- Kosher salt and black pepper
- 1 zucchini small
- 1 potato small
- Extra virgin olive oil

- 2 carrots
- 1 red bell pepper
- 3 garlic cloves
- 1 yellow onion

Method:

1. Clean the meat and sprinkle it with coarse salt and black pepper on both ends.
2. 2 tablespoons olive oil in a Dutch oven or Sauté pan over moderate flame until shimmering.
3. Cook the chicken until it is golden brown on both sides.
4. Transfer the onions, cloves, vegetables, bell peppers, sweet potato, and cabbage to the same Dutch oven.
5. Insert the tomatoes and use a rolling pin to break them up.
6. Combine the meat broth and tarragon springs in a large mixing bowl.
7. Boost the heat to high and bring the mixture to a boil.
8. Enable the chicken stew to simmer for thirty minutes over moderate flame.
9. Switch off the heat. Let the thyme sprigs out.
10. Serve with red wine vinegar and new parsley.

1.12 Lemon Chicken Piccata Recipe

Cooking Time: 50 minutes
Serving Size: 4

Ingredients:
- 3 tablespoons butter
- 2 tablespoons Italian parsley
- ¼ cup fresh lemon juice
- 2 tablespoons capers
- 3 large chicken breast

- 1 cup chicken broth
- ½ lemon
- Salt and pepper to taste
- 2 tablespoons vegetable oil
- 1 clove garlic
- ½ cup all-purpose flour

Method:
1. Preheat the oven to 200 degrees Fahrenheit.
2. To steam a covering platter, place it on the stove.
3. Dredge the grilled chicken parts in flour after seasoning them with salt and pepper.
4. Remove any extra flour by shaking it off.
5. In a pan, heat the olive oil and cook the chicken breasts until lightly brown on both sides, around 3 minutes per hand.
6. In a pan, heat and mix the chopped garlic until moist, about 20 seconds.
7. Transfer the chicken stock to the pot.
8. Bring the water to a boil after adding the lime juice. Cook for another five minutes after adding the lemon juice and capers.
9. Turn off the heat and set it aside from the tarragon.
10. Serve the meat medallions on serving plates with sauce spooned over each section.

1.13 Easy Pasta Alla Norma

Cooking Time: 50 minutes
Serving Size: 4
Ingredients:
- ½ teaspoon oregano
- ¾ cup Parmesan cheese
- ½ cup fresh basil
- 1 teaspoon red pepper flakes

- ¼ teaspoon fine salt
- 8 ounces rigatoni
- 2 medium eggplants
- ¼ cup extra-virgin olive oil
- 1 batch Marinara Sauce

Method:
1. Cook the sauce according to the package directions.
2. Preheat the oven to 425 degrees Fahrenheit in the meantime.
3. Remove the end pieces from the eggplants and slice them into 12-inch thick rounds.
4. Arrange the eggplant on the baking dishes that have been lined with parchment paper.
5. Roast for 40 - 45 minutes, or until yellow and tender.
6. Add the noodles until al dente, as per package instructions, in a large pot of simmering water.
7. In a small cup, gently fold the fried eggplant into the liquid.
8. Add 1 teaspoon extra virgin olive oil, fresh herbs, and red pepper flakes.
9. Slowly pour the pasta into the sauce, along with a few tablespoons of the retained pasta braising liquid.
10. Remove about two-thirds of the cheese and set aside for garnish.

1.14 Tuna Pasta Recipe, Mediterranean-Style

Cooking Time: 10 minutes
Serving Size: 5
  Ingredients:

- 1 jalapeno pepper
- Grated Parmesan cheese
- Black pepper
- 8 pitted Kalamata olives
- Handful fresh parsley
- 1 teaspoon oregano
- ¾ lb. spaghetti
- Zest of 1 lemon
- Juice of ½ lemon
- Kosher salt
- 6 garlic cloves
- 2 5- oz. cans albacore tuna
- 1 ½ cups frozen peas
- 1 red bell pepper
- Extra virgin olive oil

Method:
1. Add one tablespoon kosher salt, 3 quarts of liquid to boil.
2. Heat the pasta al dente in hot water as per product instructions.
3. Heat 2 tablespoon extra-virgin canola oil, heated over medium-high until shimmering in a big, deep grill grate.
4. Cook, constantly flipping, for approximately five minutes with the red bell peppers.
5. Cook, regularly flipping, for thirty seconds or until seasoning is aromatic.
6. Toss the pasta with the peas in the bowl to blend.
7. Combine the tuna, lime zest, lime juice, tarragon, marjoram, black pepper, Kalamata olives, Poblano pepper if using, and a generous amount of Parmesan cheese in a large mixing bowl.
8. To serve, divide the tuna pasta among serving bowls.

1.15 Simple Italian Minestrone Soup

Cooking Time: 1 hour 5 minutes
Serving Size: 6

Ingredients:
- 2 teaspoons lemon juice
- Parmesan cheese
- 1 can beans
- 2 cups baby spinach
- 4 tablespoons olive oil
- Freshly ground black pepper
- 1 cup whole grain orecchiette
- 2 bay leaves
- Pinch of red pepper flakes
- 2 cups water
- 1 teaspoon fine sea salt
- 1 medium yellow onion
- 1 large can of diced tomatoes
- 4 cups vegetable broth
- 2 medium carrots
- ½ teaspoon oregano
- ½ teaspoon thyme
- 2 medium ribs celery
- 2 cups seasonal vegetables
- 4 cloves garlic
- ¼ cup tomato paste

Method:
1. In a wide Dutch oven or sauté pan, heat three tablespoons of vegetable oil over moderate flame.

2. Add the remaining onion, carrot, carrots, tomato sauce, and a pinch of salt until the oil is glinting. Pan, mixing often.
3. Combine the seasonal veggies, garlic, marjoram, and thyme in a large mixing bowl.
4. In a large mixing bowl, add the pureed tomatoes, their liquids, broth, and water.
5. Combine the salt, garlic cloves, and red pepper flakes in a mixing bowl.
6. Take the water to a boil over a moderate flame, then loosely cover the pot with the cover.
7. Combine the pasta, peas, and greens in a large mixing bowl.
8. Remove the basil leaves after removing the pot from the flame.
9. Combine the lime juice and the leftover tablespoon of olive oil in a mixing bowl.
10. Serve the soup in bowls with grated Parmesan cheese on top.

1.16 Easy Biscotti Recipe with Pistachios

Cooking Time: 58 minutes
Serving Size: 36 cookies
Ingredients:
- 1 cup coarsen pistachios
- Sanding sugar
- 1 teaspoon vanilla extract
- 1 cup sweetened cranberries
- 2 cups all-purpose flour
- ¼ teaspoon salt
- 4 large eggs
- ½ teaspoon baking powder
- 1 cup sugar
Method:
1. Preheat the oven to 350 degrees Fahrenheit.

2. In a mixing bowl, add flour, sugar, brown sugar, and salt.
3. Add the three eggs and vanilla extract and beat on slow speed for 30 seconds, or until just mixed.
4. Combine the cranberries and pistachios in a mixing bowl.
5. Divide the dough in half and put it on a well-floured surface.
6. Brush the leftover egg over the dough in a small tub.
7. Use sanding powder, coat the surface.
8. Bake the logs for thirty minutes or until they are secure to the touch.
9. Preheat the oven to 325 degrees Fahrenheit.
10. Transfer the logs to a baking sheet and quickly remove each into 18 pieces with a serrated knife.
11. Bake for about 10 minutes, or until the edges of the cookies begin to crisp.
12. Enable cookies to cool absolutely on wire racks.

1.17 Easy Chicken Cacciatore Recipe

Cooking Time: 40 minutes
Serving Size: 6
Ingredients:
- ¾ cup chicken broth
- Fresh basil

- 14.5 oz. diced tomato
- ½ cup red wine
- 4 chicken breasts
- 4 cloves garlic
- 2 teaspoons rosemary
- Salt, to taste
- 1 white onion
- 1 red bell pepper
- 3 tablespoons oil
- 1 lb. Portobello mushroom
- Pepper, to taste

Method:
1. Dress both sides of the chicken thighs with salt and black pepper.
2. Four chicken parts should be seared in a skillet until lightly browned.
3. Mix in the mushrooms for about ten minutes.
4. Put the mushrooms on a tray and toss them aside.
5. In the same pan, heat and cook one tablespoon of olive oil.
6. Sprinkle with salt the vegetables and bell peppers.
7. Two minutes, stirring regularly till the vegetables and peppers have hardened.
8. Stir in the garlic and herbs until the garlic has become fragrant.
9. Mix in the onions, red wine, and stock until the liquid has lightly browned.
10. Return the mushrooms and poultry to the sauces and reduce to low heat.

1.18 Ribollita (Tuscan White Bean Soup)

Cooking Time: 1 hour
Serving Size: 3

Ingredients:
- ¼ cup Parmesan cheese
- Sea salt and black pepper
- 4 thick stale ciabatta bread
- 4 cups vegetable broth
- 3 large lacinato kale leaves
- Balsamic vinegar
- 2 tablespoons white wine
- 3 medium Roma tomatoes
- ½ teaspoon red pepper flakes
- 1 tablespoon rosemary
- 2 garlic cloves
- 1½ cups cannellini beans
- 1 small onion
- 3 carrots
- 2 tablespoons olive oil

Method:
1. In a wide saucepan over medium heat, heat the oil.
2. Cook with the onion and a tablespoon of salt and pepper.
3. Combine the vegetables, thyme, and garlic in a mixing bowl.
4. Cook for an additional four minutes.
5. Add the onions, red pepper flakes, and a sprinkle of salt to taste.
6. Cook for about fifteen minutes, just until the tomatoes are soft and ripe, stirring occasionally. Cook for a few minutes after adding the wine.
7. After that, add the peas and the vegetable broth.
8. Cook for 30 minutes to an hour or until the vegetables are tender.
9. Combine the kale, cut into cubes bread, and rain of balsamic vinegar in a mixing bowl.

10. Cook for a few more moments or until the kale has wilted.
11. Season with salt and pepper to taste, and serve immediately in large bowls.
12. Fresh Parmesan pieces should be shaved on top.

1.19 Eggplant Lasagna Recipe

Cooking Time: 1 hour 30 minutes
Serving Size: 4

Ingredients:
- ¼ cup fresh parsley
- 4 cup mozzarella
- ½ cup Parmesan
- 1 large egg
- 2 medium eggplants
- 1 25-oz. jar marinara
- 16 oz. whole milk ricotta
- Kosher salt
- 2 teaspoon oregano
- black pepper
- 3 cloves garlic
- 1 yellow onion
- 1 tablespoon olive oil

Method:
1. Preheat the oven to 400 degrees Fahrenheit.
2. Add the oil to a large frying pan.
3. After 1 minute, add the garlic, peppers, and marjoram to the plate.
4. Heat until vegetables are translucent, seasoning with salt and black pepper. Cook until the marinara has cooked through.

5. Combine gnocchi, Parmesan, cheese, and tarragon in a medium mixing bowl. Season to taste.
6. Apply a thin layer of marinara in a soup pot, then a double layer of eggplant "pasta," a layer of ricotta mixture, and a pesto layer; repeat levels.
7. Finish with marinara, chorizo, and Parmesan cheese on the last layer of eggplant.
8. Wrap in foil and cook for thirty minutes, then serve garnished with rosemary.

1.20 Mediterranean Garlic Shrimp Pasta Recipe

Cooking Time: 10 minutes
Serving Size: 4

Ingredients:
- 3 ripe vine tomatoes
- Parmesan cheese
- 1 lemon zested and juiced
- Large handful of fresh parsley
- ¾ lb. thin spaghetti
- ½ teaspoon red pepper flakes
- 1 cup dry white wine
- Kosher salt
- 5 garlic cloves
- 1 teaspoon dry oregano
- Extra virgin olive oil
- Black pepper
- ½ red onion
- 1 lb. large shrimp

Method:
1. Add the noodles as per the package instructions in lightly salted water.
2. Heat the seafood while the pasta is baking.

3. One tablespoon additional olive oil, heated in a wide large frying pan until glinting but not burning.
4. Cook the seafood for two or three minutes on each hand.
5. Onions, ginger, marjoram, and red pepper flakes should be sautéed.
6. Scrape up any bits of garlic and onions from the bottom of the pan with the wine. Then squeeze in the lemon zest and juice.
7. Toss in the tomato and minced parsley for about up to 60 seconds.
8. Toss the pasta in the skillet to coat it.
9. Add the chopped shrimp last.
10. Finish with a sprinkling of grated cheese and garlic powder.

Chapter 2: Traditional Spanish Dishes

2.1 Easy Spanish Tortilla Recipe

Cooking Time: 50 minutes
Serving Size: 4

Ingredients:
- 8 eggs, beaten
- Handful flat-leaf parsley
- 400g waxy potatoes
- 6 garlic cloves
- 4 tablespoon olive oil
- 25g butter
- 1 large white onion

To Serve
- 4 vine tomatoes
- Drizzle of olive oil
- 1 baguette

Method:
1. Preheat a large nonstick deep fryer to medium.
2. Steadily roast the onion in the butter and oil until it is tender. Slice the tomatoes in the meantime.
3. Add the potatoes to the skillet, wrap, and cook for another 15-20 minutes, occasionally mixing to ensure even cooking.
4. Add 2 garlic cloves crushed and mixed in, followed by pounded eggs.
5. Replace the lid on the pan and bake the tortilla on low heat.
6. When the tortilla is finished, move it to a plate and eat it warm or hot, with grated parmesan on top.

2.2 Mediterranean-Style Steamed Clams Recipe

Cooking Time: 1 hour
Serving Size: 4
Ingredients:
- 1 green onion
- ⅓ cup parsley
- 1 ½ cup water
- 3 pounds littleneck clams
- Extra virgin olive oil
- ½ teaspoon red pepper flakes
- 1 cup dry white wine
- 1 yellow onion
- ½ teaspoon cumin
- ½ teaspoon smoked paprika
- ½ green pepper
- Salt and pepper
- 2 ripe tomatoes
- 4 garlic cloves minced
- ½ red pepper

Method:
1. Clams should be cleaned.
2. Put down the clams in the first container of cool simmering water for about 20 minutes.
3. To make the red wine soup, add all of the ingredients to a big mixing bowl.
4. ¼ cup olive oil, heated in a big Dutch oven over moderate flame.
5. Combine the onions, tomatoes, and garlic in a large mixing bowl.
6. Cook for five minutes after seasoning with kosher salt and black pepper.
7. Add the onions, smoked paprika, parmesan, and garlic powder, and stir to combine.

8. Combine the white wine and liquid in a mixing bowl.
9. Process for a few minutes, just until the tomato is slightly softened.
10. In a red wine sauce, heat the clams.
11. Reduce the heat to medium-low and add the clams.
12. Cook, covered until the remainder of the clams has opened.
13. Switch off the heat. Combine the spring onions and parsley in a mixing bowl.

2.3 Gambas al Ajillo (Spanish Garlic Shrimp)

Cooking Time: 20 minutes
Serving Size: 4
Ingredients:
- 2 tablespoons dry sherry
- 1 tablespoon Italian parsley
- 1 teaspoon hot smoked paprika
- ¼ cup extra-virgin olive oil
- 1 pound shrimp
- 4 cloves garlic

Method:
1. Finely cut garlic. Paprika and sea salt are used to season the shrimp. To coat, mix it.
2. In a pan, cook the garlic and oil on moderate flame.
3. Cook for about two minutes or until the garlic begins to turn translucent.
4. Increase the heat to the extreme and add the shrimp.
5. Toss and rotate the shrimp with tongs for around two minutes or until they start to curl but are still uncooked.

6. Pour the sherry in. Heat, constantly stirring, for 1 minute more, or till sauces come to boiling and shrimp is fried through.
7. Remove the pan from the heat. With a spoon, fold in the parsley.

2.4 20-Minute Couscous Recipe with Shrimp and Chorizo

Cooking Time: 25 minutes
Serving Size: 6
Ingredients:
- Boiling water
- 1 cup fresh parsley
- 1.5 lb. large shrimp
- 1 ¼ cup couscous
- 1 ¼ teaspoon ground cumin
- Salt
- 1 ¼ teaspoon turmeric
- 1 ¼ teaspoon paprika
- 6 oz. hard Spanish Chorizo
- 3 garlic cloves
- 2 jalapeno peppers
- 1 small yellow onion
- Extra virgin olive

Method:
1. Heat a small amount of vegetable oil in a large frying pan.
2. Heat the Chorizo sausage rolls until they are crisp.
3. Remove from the heat and clean on towels.
4. Add the garlic, onions, and habanero to the boiling pot and cook till the vegetables are transparent.

5. Now insert the seasoning and mix for a few seconds before adding the shrimp.
6. Heat the shrimp for approximately 3 minutes on moderate flame.
7. In the meantime, bring 2 ½ cups of water to a boil.
8. Transfer the couscous, little more vegetable oil, a pinch of salt, and the hot oil to the frying pan with the Chorizo.
9. Allow for five minutes of resting time. Remove the cover and add the fresh parsley.
10.   Enjoy by moving to serve pots.

2.5 One Pan Spanish Chicken and Rice Recipe with Chorizo

Cooking Time: 1 hour
Serving Size: 5
Ingredients:
For Chicken
- 3 tablespoon tomato paste
- 3 cups chicken broth
- 2 garlic cloves
- 1 large ripe tomato
- 1 ½ cup rice
- 1 large green bell pepper
- 1 medium red onion
- 4 chicken thighs
- Olive oil
- 6 oz. bulk chorizo sausage
- 4 chicken drumsticks
For Spice Rub
- 1 teaspoon black pepper
- ½ teaspoon cayenne pepper
- 1 teaspoon garlic powder

- 1 teaspoon salt
- 1 tablespoon smoked paprika

Method:
1. Soak the grain in water for a few minutes.
2. Position the rice in a bowl after thoroughly rinsing it.
3. Combine the ingredients, salt, and peppers in a small cup.
4. Dress the chicken with salt and pepper.
5. Both sides of the chicken should be browned.
6. Cautiously put the chicken in the pot and cook both sides thoroughly.
7. Transfer the chorizo to the same plate.
8. Combine the green beans, onions, and garlic in a large mixing bowl.
9. Cook for five minutes over a moderate flame, stirring frequently.
10. Combine the sliced tomatoes, tomato sauce, and chicken stock in a large mixing b
11. owl. Return the browned poultry to the bowl. Cook for 20 to 30 minutes at 350°F.
12. Cook the rice in the same pot as the chicken.
13. Allow the chicken and rice to rest in the pan for a few minutes.

2.6 Easy Seafood Paella Recipe

Cooking Time: 1 hour
Serving Size: 6

Ingredients:
- 1 lb. prawns
- ¼ cup fresh parsley

- 2 large Roma tomatoes
- 6 oz. French green beans
- 4 small lobster tails
- ½ teaspoon chili pepper flakes
- Salt
- Water
- 1 teaspoon Spanish paprika
- 1 teaspoon cayenne pepper
- 3 tablespoon olive oil
- 4 garlic cloves
- 2 large pinches of saffron
- 2 cups Spanish rice
- 1 large yellow onion

Method:
1. Take 3 cups of water to a gentle simmer in a big saucepan.
2. Tongs are used to cut the lobster tails.
3. After 2 minutes of sautéing the onions, add the garlic and cook for another 3 minutes, stirring frequently.
4. Combine the saffron, dripping water, paprika, smoked paprika, Aleppo paprika, and salt in a mixing bowl.
5. Combine the tomato slices and green beans in a mixing bowl.
6. Cook for an additional ten minutes, just until the seafood changes color.
7. Add the cooked seafood chunks last.
8. Serve with rosemary as a garnish.
9. With your favorite white wine, eat the paella sweet.

2.7 Spanish Tuna and Potato Salad Recipe

Cooking Time: 24 minutes

Serving Size: 8

Ingredients:
- 3 tablespoon white wine vinegar
- 6 oz. spring greens
- ½ teaspoon red pepper flakes
- ⅓ cup Greek olive oil
- 1 teaspoon smoked paprika
- ¾ teaspoon cumin
- 3 large garlic cloves
- Salt and pepper
- 12 oz. fingerling potatoes
- ⅓ cup pearl red onions
- 15 oz. can quality tuna
- 6 oz. small tomatoes
- 10 oz. French green beans

Method:
1. Fill a big pot halfway with water and add the fingerling vegetables.
2. Cook for ten minutes at a low temperature.
3. Fill a wide bowl halfway with ice water and place it next to the pot.
4. Green beans should be added to the hot water in the same frying pan.
5. Cook for about four minutes.
6. Wash the green beans and instantly placed them in the ice water bowl.
7. Green beans, peppers, tomatoes, fish, and garlic are added to the pot.
8. Add Salt, powder, parmesan, cumin, and ground red pepper to taste.
9. Toss all together gently to ensure that all of the components are properly coated.
10. Taste and change seasoning, if necessary, by adding more smoked paprika, cilantro, or smashed red pepper.

2.8 Easy Tomato Gazpacho Recipe

Cooking Time: 15 minutes
Serving Size: 6
Ingredients:
- A small handful of mint leaves
- Small cilantro leaves
- 5 slices stale artisan bread
- 1 teaspoon cayenne pepper
- Pinch sugar
- Water
- Salt and pepper
- ½ teaspoon cumin
- 5 large ripe tomatoes
- Olive oil
- 2 tablespoon sherry vinegar
- ½ English cucumber
- 2 green onions
- 2 garlic cloves
- 1 green pepper
- 1 celery stalk

Method:
1. In a pan, combine the bread slices and ½ cup of water.
2. Remove the tops of the tomatoes.
3. Combine the tomatoes, carrots, fennel, green beans, fresh basil, and garlic in a big blender or food processor.
4. Place the soaking bread on top.
5. Pour ½ cup olive oil and sherry wine into a mixing bowl.
6. If the gazpacho is too thick, add more water and mix again until consistency is right.
7. Fill a glass beaker or wide canning jar with the mixture.

8. Cover tightly with plastic wrap and place in the refrigerator to cool.
9. Offer the gazpacho a short swirl before transferring it to serving bowls or small glasses.

2.9 Mediterranean Wrap

Cooking Time: 10 minutes
Serving Size: 1
Ingredients:
- 2 tablespoons basil pesto
- 1-2 tablespoons feta cheese
- ¼ cup rotisserie chicken
- 3 tablespoons tomatoes
- 1 cow cheese wedge
- ½ cup greens lettuce
- 1 tortilla wrap

Method:
1. Place the tortilla on a flat surface and scatter the Laughing Cow cheesy wedge down the middle.
2. Insert the mixed greens just to the side of the cheese.
3. Cover with the meat, sun-dried vegetables, and pesto, spooned on top and softly spread.
4. Over the risotto, break the gruyere cheese.
5. Fold the upper part of the tortilla inwards somewhat, then roll it up tightly.
6. Break the wrap in half with a sharp knife and eat right away!

2.10 Rice Spanish Vegetables Recipe

Cooking Time: 45 minutes
Serving Size: 8
Ingredients:
- ½ teaspoon salt

- Chopped cilantro
- 2 teaspoons cumin
- 1 teaspoon chili powder
- ¾ cup corn kernels
- ½ cup peas
- 3 tablespoons olive oil
- 1 cup tomatoes
- 2 2/3 cups vegetable broth
- 1 small onion
- 1½ cups white rice
- 1 tablespoon tomato paste
- 1 large carrot
- 3 cloves garlic
- 1 medium green pepper

Method:
1. In a medium saucepan, heat the oil on moderate flame.
2. Add the onion, garlic, and carrots to the hot oil.
3. Cook for an additional minute, just until the vegetables have softened.
4. Cook for thirty seconds, just until the garlic is fragrant. Toss in the rice.
5. Mix in the chopped tomatoes, then insert the tomatoes, stock, corn, peas, cumin, chili powder, and salt to taste.
6. Remove the rice from the heat and set it aside for ten minutes, covered.
7. Toss the rice with a spoon to fluff it up.
8. Taste and sprinkle with more salt if necessary, then top with coriander.

2.11 Summer Spanish Salad

Cooking Time: 10 minutes
Serving Size: 2

Ingredients:
- 3 tablespoons olive oil
- 2 tablespoon red wine vinegar
- A pinch of cumin
- ½ teaspoon salt
- 2 large tomatoes
- 1 large green pepper
- 2 cloves garlic minced
- 1 medium onion
- 1 large cucumber

Method:
1. Dip the onions in water after cutting them into small cubes.
2. Position the tomatoes, celery, and peppers in a cup and chop them up.
3. Drain the vegetables and combine them with the remaining ingredients.
4. In a separate small cup, combine the remaining olive oil, vinegar, and salt, then stir in the garlic paste.
5. Toss the salad with the dressing and toss well.
6. Cover and store in the refrigerator.

2.12 Saucy Spanish Chicken with Green Olives

Cooking Time: 150 minutes
Serving Size: 8

Ingredients:
- ¼ cup sherry
- 1 tablespoon cornstarch
- 2 teaspoon dried thyme
- 1 teaspoon cumin and paprika
- 8 chicken drumsticks
- 1 small red onion

- 2 large garlic cloves
- 1 cup green olives
- 389ml can tomato sauce

Method:
1. Remove the skin from the chicken and remove any excess fat.
2. Pour the sauce in. Quantify out the artichokes, then cut them up and throw them in.
3. Combine the onion, ginger, thyme, smoked paprika, and tarragon in a mixing bowl.
4. Place the chicken in the paste to coat it, then turn it bone-side out. Push your way into the liquid.
5. Cook for six hours on medium or 2½ to 3 hours on average, or until chicken reaches 165°F.
6. Combine cornstarch and a few tablespoons of water in a mixing bowl and whisk until smooth.
7. Stir frequently in the sauce until it thickens, around five minutes. Chicken should be served over rice.

2.13 Mediterranean Seafood Stew

Cooking Time: 45 minutes
Serving Size: 6

Ingredients:
- 3 tablespoon toasted pine nuts
- Crusty Italian bread
- 2 lb. skinless sea bass fillet
- ½ cup fresh parsley leaves
- Olive oil
- ¼ cup golden raisins
- 2 tablespoon capers
- 1 large yellow onion
- 1 28-oz. can plum tomatoes

- 3 cups vegetable broth
- Pinch red pepper flakes
- ¾ cup dry white wine
- 2 celery ribs
- 4 large garlic cloves
- ½ teaspoon dried thyme
- Salt and pepper

Method:

1. 1 tablespoon olive oil, heated over moderate flame.
2. Add the onions, fennel, and a pinch of salt and pepper to taste.
3. Cook for a few minutes until the thyme, red pepper flakes, and cloves are aromatic.
4. Decrease the fluid by about ½ percent by getting it to a simmer.
5. Combine the peppers, vegetable broth, pecans, and chives in a large mixing bowl.
6. Cook for 15-20 minutes over a moderate flame, stirring periodically until the flavors have melded.
7. Place the fish parts in the liquid ingredients and gently stir them all together. Cover the Dutch oven and turn off the heat.
8. Mix in the chopped parsley last.
9. Fill serving bowls halfway with the spicy fish stew.

2.14 Rustic Spanish Chicken Casserole

Cooking Time: 1 hour 20 minutes
Serving Size: 6
Ingredients:
- ½ teaspoon cayenne pepper
- 1 cup basil leaves
- 1 teaspoon dried oregano
- ½ teaspoon smoked paprika
- 1 cup stuffed pimento olives
- 1 carrot, diced
- 1 red bell pepper
- 2 tablespoon tomato paste
- 1 can cannellini beans
- ½ cup chicken stock
- 1 tablespoon olive oil
- 8 chicken thigh cutlets
- 2 cans tomatoes
- 3 garlic cloves
- 1 white onion

Method:
1. Preheat the oven to 180 degrees Celsius.
2. In a huge slow cooker, heat the oil over moderate flame.
3. For a few minutes, sauté the cloves and vegetables until they are translucent.
4. Cook for a few minutes after adding the chicken thighs.
5. With the exception of the basil leaves, combine all of the remaining ingredients in a mixing bowl.
6. 5 minutes on top of the burner, heat until softly bubbling.
7. Preheat the oven to 350°F and bake for 45 minutes on average.

8. Serve with carrots or cabbage rice.

2.15 Mediterranean Skillet Chicken with Bulgur Paella, Carrots

Cooking Time: 50 minutes
Serving Size: 4
Ingredients:
Lemon Yogurt Sauce
- Pinch of cayenne pepper
- Kosher salt
- Zest and juice of 1 lemon
- 2 tablespoons curly parsley
- 1½ cups plain yogurt

For the Chicken
- ½ cup golden raisins
- ½ cup curly parsley sprigs
- 2 cups safflower oil
- ½ cup whole blanched almonds
- 6 chicken thighs
- 2 bay leaves
- 1½ cups basmati rice
- 4 whole cloves
- 2 cinnamon sticks
- 3 cups chicken stock
- 5 cardamom pods
- 6 chicken drumsticks
- 2 tablespoons tomato paste
- 3 strips orange zest
- Kosher salt and pepper
- ½ teaspoon turmeric
- 2 tomatoes
- 2 tablespoons olive oil
- 1 teaspoon cumin

- 1 teaspoon coriander
- 1 large onion
- 2 teaspoons fresh ginger
- ½ cup grated carrot
- 3 cloves garlic

Method:
1. Combine yogurt, lime juice and zest, tarragon, and smoked paprika in a medium mixing cup.
2. Put aside after seasoning with salt.
3. Preheat the oven to 375 degrees Fahrenheit.
4. Season the chicken with salt and pepper before serving.
5. Reduce the heat to medium-low and add the spices.
6. Place them skin-side up golden brown chicken in the boiling liquid and bake for 25 minutes.
7. Take the rice to a boil in a saucepan with the stored liquid ingredients over moderate flame.
8. Stir in the rice, cover, and cook on low heat until the rice is tender about 20 minutes.

2.16 Pisto (Spanish Vegetable Stew)

Cooking Time: 1 hour 20 minutes
Serving Size: 8
Ingredients:
- 1 teaspoon honey
- 2 medium zucchini
- 1.5 cans tomatoes
- 1.5 teaspoons salt
- 1 green bell pepper
- 2 garlic cloves
- 1 large eggplant
- ½ long red chili
- 1 red bell pepper

- Good quality olive oil
- 1 large onion
- ½ teaspoon salt

Method:
1. Spray the eggplant with salts and slice it into pieces.
2. Allow for 15-20 minutes of rest time.
3. In a big, roasting pan, heat four tablespoons of canola oil over moderate flame.
4. Combine the onions, chili, and diced beans in a large mixing bowl. Cook for 12-14 minutes over moderate flame.
5. Fry for 4-5 minutes, mixing halfway through, until the eggplant is golden brown.
6. Remove the eggplant from the pan and drizzle with a little more canola oil.
7. Cook for another 4-5 minutes after adding the zucchini.
8. Ultimately, mix in the pre-fried zucchini and eggplant to the tomatoes concentrate in the pot.
9. Cover and cook for 25 minutes over a moderate flame with a seal.

2.17 Spanish Orange & Olive Salad

Cooking Time: 20 minutes
Serving Size: 4

Ingredients:
For the Softened Leeks
- ¼ teaspoon kosher salt
- 1 tablespoon water
- 1 tablespoon white wine vinegar
- 1 small leek

For the Orange & Olive Salad
- Squeeze lemon juice
- ¼ cup Marcona almonds

- Sprinkle flaky sea salt
- Sprinkle Sumac
- 6 oranges
- 4 teaspoon leek vinegar marinade
- 1 tablespoon olive oil
- 3 tablespoon softened leeks
- ⅓ cup halved olives

Method:

1. To begin, prepare and marinate the leeks.
2. Cut the white color green pieces into rounds with a thin knife.
3. 1 tablespoon balsamic vinegar syrup, sea salt, and 1 tablespoon water are combined with the leeks.
4. Allow fifteen minutes for the leeks to caramelize, tossing periodically.
5. Cut the oranges into circles after segmenting them.
6. Cast aside half of the olives.
7. In a medium mixing bowl, combine the bananas, olives, and 3 tablespoons of the brined leeks.
8. Toss in 4 teaspoons of the leek marinade and 4 teaspoons of olive oil in a mixing bowl softly.
9. Add a pinch of flaky sea salt, sumac, a splash of lime juice, and nuts to the salad.
10. Serve directly after garnishing.

2.18 Mediterranean Olive Toss

Cooking Time: 45 minutes
Serving Size: 8

Ingredients:

- 2 cups spinach leaves

- ½ cup feta cheese
- 7 pickled red peppers
- ¼ cup Kalamata olives
- 1 package penne pasta
- 4 large cloves of garlic
- 1 (8 ounces) jar artichoke
- ⅓ cup olive oil

Method:
1. Fill a large pot halfway with liquid and bring to the boil, lightly toasted.
2. Return to a boil after adding the penne.
3. Heat pasta for ten minutes, covered, then rinse.
4. In a large skillet over medium heat, heat the olive oil on moderate heat and cook and mix garlic once aromatic, around 30 seconds.
5. 5 minutes after adding the pine nuts, tomatoes, and artichokes to the skillet, stir to combine flavors.
6. Remove from the heat and stir in the penne pasta until well combined; toss the pasta mixture gently with the feta cheese.

2.19 Mediterranean Basa Stew & Sunny Aioli

Cooking Time: 1 hour
Serving Size: 2

Ingredients:
- 1 white wine vinegar
- 1 carrot
- 1 garlic clove
- 1 tomato paste
- 2 ciabatta rolls
- 1 mayonnaise
- 1 garlic clove
- 1 vegetable stock

- 1 brown onion
- 1 teaspoon ground turmeric
- 5g parsley
- 2 x 100g basa fillets
- 1-star anise
- 1 bag of pitted black olives

Method:
1. Preheat the oven to 220 degrees Celsius.
2. Using a drizzle of canola oil, heat a big, wide-based pan.
3. Insert the chopped onion, sliced carrot, and a quarter of the garlic once the pan is warmed.
4. Heat for 6-8 minutes, just until the onions are soft and transparent, after adding the star anise.
5. Whisk together the mayo, the leftover minced garlic, the red wine vinegar, and add salt and pepper.
6. Place the ciabatta rolls on a baking sheet and bake them for 8-10 minutes.
7. Warm a drizzle of olive oil in a separate wide broad pan over medium temperature.
8. When the pan is warmed, skin-side up, add the sea bass, and boil for four minutes.
9. With the warm ciabatta on the side, place the grilled sea bass over the soup.

2.20 Spanish Style Albondigas

Cooking Time: 2 hours 20 minutes
Serving Size: 4

Ingredients:
- 1 can plum tomatoes
- 2 tablespoons olive oil
- 1 cup white wine
- 2 tablespoons tomato puree

- ¼ teaspoon coriander
- 2 grinds black pepper
- ⅔ pound beef
- 1 ½ teaspoons basil
- 1 ½ teaspoons oregano
- ⅓ pound pork
- 2 tablespoons celery
- 1 clove garlic
- 2 tablespoons carrot
- 3 ½ ounces pancetta
- 3 tablespoons onion
- 3 ½ ounces white bread crumbs
- 2 tablespoons olive oil
- 2 tablespoons red bell pepper
- 2 dashes Worcestershire sauce
- Salt and pepper
- 2 tablespoons green onion
- 1 tablespoon fresh parsley
- 1 clove garlic
- 2 tablespoons fresh oregano

Method:
1. In a mixing bowl, combine ground beef, pork belly, spring onions, oregano, tarragon, garlic, Balsamic vinegar, salt, and black pepper.
2. Slowly stir in the breadcrumbs until the meat mixture reaches the perfect consistency.
3. Freezer meatballs for at least 30 minutes after wrapping them in cling film.
4. In a big saucepan, steam 2 tablespoons olive oil on medium-high heat.
5. In a hot skillet, continue cooking pancetta until it is golden brown, about four minutes. Toss in the vegetables and seasoning.
6. In a wide skillet, steam 2 tablespoons of oil over medium heat.

7. 6 to 10 minutes, continue cooking meatballs in hot oil quantities until uniformly browned and heated through.
8. Transfer the meatballs softly into the boiling sauce and cook together until the meatballs are thoroughly cooked.

Chapter 3: Traditional French Dishes

3.1 Ratatouille

Cooking Time: 40 minutes
Serving Size: 8

Ingredients:
Veggies
- 2 yellow squashes
- 2 zucchinis
- 6 Roma tomatoes
- 2 eggplants

Sauce
- 28 oz. can of tomatoes
- 2 tablespoons fresh basil
- Salt, to taste
- Pepper, to taste
- 2 tablespoons olive oil
- 1 red bell pepper
- 1 yellow bell pepper
- 4 cloves garlic
- 1 onion

Herb Seasoning
- Pepper, to taste
- 4 tablespoons olive oil
- 2 teaspoons fresh thyme
- Salt, to taste
- 1 teaspoon garlic
- 2 tablespoons fresh parsley
- 2 tablespoons fresh basil

Method:
1. Preheat the oven to 375 degrees Fahrenheit.
2. Cut the eggplant, onions, squash, and sweet potato into thin slices.

3. In a 12-inch stove pan, heat the oil over moderate flame.
4. Sauté the onion, cloves, and bell pepper for about ten minutes, or until soft.
5. Combine the basil, ginger, garlic, tarragon, salt, vinegar, and balsamic vinegar in a small cup.
6. Season the veggies with the herb spice.
7. Bake for thirty minutes with the pan wrapped in foil.
8. Serve as a side dish or main course while still hot.

3.2 Mediterranean Veggie Sauté

Cooking Time: 15 minutes
Serving Size: 4
Ingredients:
- ⅛ teaspoon garlic powder
- ⅛ teaspoon Sicilian sea salt
- 2 teaspoons olive oil
- ¼ teaspoon sugar
- 2 medium zucchini
- 2 teaspoons Greek seasoning
- 2 teaspoons balsamic vinegar
- 1 small red bell pepper
- 1 medium yellow onion

Method:
1. On moderate flame, heat a large Sautee pan sprayed with cooking spray until warm.
2. Cook and mix for 6 minutes until either zucchini, onions, and bell pepper are caramelized on the edges.
3. In a small cup, combine the rest of the ingredients.
4. Switch off the heat in the skillet. Toss in the spice mixture softly to coat.

3.3 French Mediterranean-Style Fish Soup

Cooking Time: 40 minutes
Serving Size: 6

Ingredients:
The Fish Broth

- 6 fresh thyme
- A 2-inch strip of orange zest
- 1 fennel bulb
- 1 medium-size onion
- 3 tablespoons olive oil
- 6 garlic cloves
- 8 pounds whole fish

The Soup Base

- ½-inch French baguette
- 2 cups garlic mayonnaise
- 8 medium-size tomatoes
- ¼ cup Pernod
- 3 tablespoons olive oil
- 3 medium-size leeks

Method:
1. Fill a pot halfway with ice water and soak the fish bones and faces for at least 30 minutes.
2. In a 4-quart bath, heat 3 tablespoons of canola oil.
3. Combine the garlic, fennel, onion, spices, and lime zest in a large mixing bowl. Cook, boiling periodically, over medium-high heat.
4. Mix in the veggies with a rolling pin for another ten minutes or until they begin to fall apart.
5. Remove the bones and veggies and toss them out.
6. Heat the leeks softly in the olive oil for about ten minutes or until they soften and become somewhat transparent.

7. Bake the bread slices under the grill just before eating the stew.

3.4 Mediterranean French bread Pizza

Cooking Time: 50 minutes
Serving Size: 4
Ingredients:
- 2 ounces goat cheese
- 4 fresh basil leaves
- 2 ounces provolone
- 2 ounces feta
- 1 12 inch loaf bread
- ¼ teaspoon black pepper
- 2 ounces mozzarella
- 10 ounces heavy pizza sauce
- 4 ounces of a portabella mushroom
- ½ teaspoon salt
- 1 fire-roasted red pepper
- 8 ounces of baby spinach
- 1-ounce olive oil
- 6 ounces artichoke hearts
- 2 cloves garlic

Method:
1. The loaf of bread should be split in half longways.
2. On both halves of the crust, distribute the pizza sauce.
3. Artichoke cores, mushrooms, and roast bell pepper are sautéed in a hot pan with canola oil, followed by spinach, garlic powder, and pepper.
4. Cover the sauces with the hot mixture that has been split between the French toast's two halves.

5. Bake for four to five minutes at 400°F in a preheated pan or your bread oven.
6. Take the pizza from the microwave and scatter the basil leaves on top.

3.5 Soupe au Pistou

Cooking Time: 2 hours 30 minutes
Serving Size: 6

Ingredients:
For the Soup

- ½ cup soup pasta
- Freshly ground pepper
- 2 medium-size turnips
- ½ pound green beans
- 2 celery stalks
- 1 medium-size zucchini
- 1 ½ cups white beans
- 2 cups green cabbage
- 2 large carrots
- 1 large onion
- 2 leeks
- 1 pound tomatoes
- Salt to taste
- 1 tablespoon olive oil
- 4 large garlic cloves

For the Pistou

- Freshly ground pepper
- ½ cup Parmesan
- ⅓ cup extra virgin olive oil
- ½ cup grated Parmesan
- 2 large garlic cloves
- 2 cups fresh basil leaves
- Salt to taste

Method:

1. In a big, heavy casserole dish or Dutch oven, pour the white beans and add 2 quarts of liquid. Get the water to a boil.
2. In a large skillet, heat the oil, then put the rest sliced onions and a large salt pinch. Insert the leeks and the rest of the garlic.
3. Transfer all of the leftover vegetables, except for the black beans, to the casserole dish and whisk to blend.
4. In a mixer, grind the herb a pinch at a time to a mixture, then throw the garlic back in and blend well.
5. 10 minutes before eating, add the noodles to the boiling soup and cook until al dente.
6. Season with pepper and salt to taste.
7. Warm the soup while stirring in the blanched black beans.

3.6 Sea Bass with Olives and Cherry Tomatoes

Cooking Time: 25 minutes
Serving Size: 4

Ingredients:
- 4 6-ounce fillets sea bass
- ¼ cup fresh basil
- 1 tablespoon olive oil
- Kosher salt and pepper
- 1 shallot
- 2 cups cherry tomatoes
- ½ cup green olives
- 2 garlic cloves

Method:
1. Preheat the broiler by putting a rack in the upper third of the oven.

2. In a medium mixing bowl, mix the shallot, garlic, onions, olives, and butter, sprinkle with salt, and toss properly.
3. Season the fish with salt and black pepper in a ceramic baking dish.
4. Sprinkle tomato combination over salmon and broil for 10–13 minutes, or until salmon is opaque throughout vegetables have begun to burst.
5. Serve with a sprinkling of basil on top.

3.7 Mediterranean French Lentil Salad

Cooking Time: 25 minutes
Serving Size: 6

Ingredients:
- 2 tablespoons parsley
- Lemon juice and zest
- 1/3 cup red onion
- 4 ounces feta cheese
- 2 cups French lentils
- ¾ cup cucumber
- ¾ cup Kalamata olives
- 1 cup lacinato kale
- ¾ cup tomatoes
- ¾ cup red peppers

Dressing
- ½ teaspoon oregano
- Salt and black pepper
- ½ teaspoon Dijon mustard
- ½ teaspoon maple syrup
- 1 tablespoon red wine vinegar
- 2 tablespoons olive oil

Method:
1. Position the lentils in a big saucepan after rinsing them.

2. Cover with around 6 cups of water and a bit of salt to taste.
3. Bring to the boil, reduce to low heat, and cook for twenty minutes or until lentils are soft. If required, remove the excess water.
4. In a big mixing bowl, whisk together the dressing ingredients.
5. Pour in the lentils and the rest of the components.
6. Salad can be eaten right away or kept refrigerated for up to three days.

3.8 French Cauliflower Gratin

Cooking Time: 30 minutes
Serving Size: 4
Ingredients:
- ½ cup Swiss cheese
- Salt and pepper
- 3 tablespoons flour
- 2 ½ cups milk
- 5 tablespoons butter
- 1 large head cauliflower

Method:
1. Cauliflower should be washed and cut into thin strips.
2. Cook the bits for about ten minutes in a big pot of water.
3. Preheat the oven to 350 degrees Fahrenheit.
4. Heat the oil in a saucepan over medium heat to make the béchamel.
5. Mix in the flour with vigor. You will get a dense cream-like substance.
6. Then, when proceeding to combine with the whisk, slowly add the milk.

7. Drop the béchamel over the cabbage, sprinkle with the leftover cream parmesan, and bake for thirty minutes, exposed.

3.9 Mediterranean Fish Soup with Garlicky Rouille

Cooking Time: 2 hours 30 minutes
Serving Size: 8
Ingredients:
- Pinch of dried oregano
- ½ cup Parmesan cheese
- 1 pound tuna
- 1 small baguette
- 1 gold potato
- 1½ pounds monkfish
- 1 pound skinless cod fillet
- 16 garlic cloves
- 12 thyme sprigs
- Freshly ground pepper
- 1 cup dry white wine
- 2 quarts fish stock
- 1½ cups olive oil
- ⅛ teaspoon saffron threads
- 3 tablespoons tomato paste
- Salt
- ½ tablespoon ground cumin
- ½ teaspoon sweet paprika
- ½ tablespoon pepper
- ½ tablespoon fennel seeds
- ¼ teaspoon cayenne pepper
- 1 celery rib
- 1 fennel bulb
- 1 large onion

- 2 large leeks

Method:

1. Heat the potato cubes in a small saucepan of lightly salted water.
2. Mash the potatoes with the stored potato water and the garlic powder until soft.
3. Preheat the oven to 350 degrees Fahrenheit.
4. Heat and cook ½ cup vegetable oil in a large casserole dish until it shimmers.
5. Cook over medium temperature with the leeks, onions, celery, chives bulb, and six doubled garlic cloves.
6. Put the soup to a boil with the fish meal and the thyme package.
7. Organize the baguette pieces on a cookie dish in the meantime.
8. Toast the baguette pieces for about five minutes until its golden brown.
9. Pour the fish soup into shallow bowls and top with a little rouille.

3.10 Mediterranean Loaded French fry Salad

Cooking Time: 45 minutes
Serving Size: 2

Ingredients:
Yogurt Sauce

- 1 teaspoon kosher salt
- 2 teaspoons lemon juice
- 1 tablespoon fresh dill
- 2 cloves garlic
- ¼ cup fresh parsley
- 1½ cups Greek yogurt

Fries

- 3 medium russet potatoes
- 1 package spice blend

- 2 cups ice
- 2 tablespoons lemon juice
- Coldwater
- 4 cups vegetable oil

Toppings
- ½ cup feta cheese
- 2 tablespoons dill
- 1 plum tomato
- ¼ cup red onion
- ½ cup cucumber
- 1 cup romaine lettuce
- ½ cup chickpeas

Method:

1. Combine the yogurt, parsley, tarragon, cloves, salt, and lime juice in a medium mixing bowl.
2. In a big mixing bowl, combine ice water, ice, and one tablespoon lime juice.
3. Slice the potatoes and cut them into 14-inch thick, 3-inch large pieces.
4. Refrigerate for thirty minutes after adding the leftover tablespoon of lime juice.
5. Heat the potato in the hot oil in groups for 5–10 minutes until it's soft and light yellow.
6. Raise the temperature of the oil to 375°F.
7. Transfer the chips to the hot oil in groups and continue to cook for 5–10 minutes, or until the light is nicely browned.
8. Pour more yogurt sauce on top. Dill should be sprinkled on top.

3.11 Ratatouille French Vegetable Stew

Cooking Time: 45 minutes
Serving Size: 4
Ingredients:

Salad

- 1/3 cup feta
- ¼ cup basil
- ½ cup artichoke hearts
- 1/3 cup Kalamata olives
- 1 cup green lentils
- ½ red bell pepper
- ½ English cucumber
- 3 cups chicken broth

Dressing

- 3 tablespoons olive oil
- Salt and black pepper
- 2 tablespoons balsamic vinegar
- 1 tablespoon lemon juice

Method:

1. Rinse the lentils and exclude any foreign material.
2. Combine with broth or water in a casserole dish.
3. In a mixing bowl, combine the warm lentils.
4. Mix the lime juice and sour cream to make the seasoning.
5. Slowly drizzle in the olive oil and season with salt and pepper to taste.
6. Combine the lentils and vinaigrette in a mixing bowl.
7. Enable to cool to room temperature before adding the remaining ingredients.

3.12 Mediterranean Chicken Marbella

Cooking Time: 4 hours 15 minutes
Serving Size: 8

Ingredients:

- ½ cup white wine
- 2 tablespoons Italian parsley
- 3 bay leaves

- ¼ cup brown sugar
- 2 chickens
- 8 Spanish green olives
- ¼ cup capers
- ½ head of garlic
- ¼ cup olive oil
- ½ cup prunes
- Coarse salt and pepper
- ¼ cup red wine vinegar
- 2 tablespoons oregano

Method:
1. Conjoin garlic, marjoram, salt, and black pepper to taste, seasoning, canola oil, prunes, artichokes, capers with water, and garlic cloves in a large mixing bowl.
2. Transfer the chicken parts to the marinade and cover absolutely.
3. Place the chicken in a baking pan and pour the marinade, brown sugar, and wine over it.
4. Preheat the oven to 350 degrees Fahrenheit.
5. Bake for 50-100 minutes, basting regularly with cooking liquid.
6. Transfer the chicken, dried apricots, olives, and dill to a baking tray using a slotted spoon.
7. Serve the chicken with a few of the cooking liquid and a generous amount of parsley.
8. In a sauceboat, serve the leftover juices.

3.13 Mediterranean Baguette

Cooking Time: 1 hour
Serving Size: 4

Ingredients:
- ½ lb. prosciutto
- Italian dressing

- Sliced mozzarella cheese
- Basil leaves
- Real mayonnaise
- Baby spinach leaves
- Sliced plum tomatoes
- 1 French baguette

Method:
1. Try squeezing arugula, onions, mozzarella, herbs, prosciutto onto a baguette, and layer with real sour cream.
2. The dressing should be drizzled on top.

3.14 Mediterranean Spinach Strata

Cooking Time: 40 minutes
Serving Size: 10
Ingredients:
- 5 large eggs
- 4 large egg whites
- 2 tablespoons Dijon mustard
- 1 ½ teaspoons oregano
- ¾ cup Asiago cheese
- 3 cups milk
- 3 cups plum tomato
- 1 (4-ounce) package feta cheese
- 2 loaves French bread baguette
- Cooking spray
- ½ teaspoon salt
- ½ teaspoon black pepper
- 1 cup onion
- 1 tablespoon all-purpose flour
- 2 (7-ounce) bags of baby spinach
- 1 package mushrooms

- 4 garlic cloves

Method:
1. Preheat the oven to 350 degrees Fahrenheit.
2. Position slices of bread on a cookie dish in a thin layer.
3. Preheat oven to 350°F and bake for ten minutes, or until golden brown.
4. Over moderate flame, brush a large sauté pan with olive oil.
5. Add the onion, garlic, and mushrooms and cook over medium heat until the mushrooms are tender. Toss in the spinach container.
6. Top with sliced tomatoes, feta cheese, and a quarter of the Asiago cheese.
7. Place the leftover bread slices on top of the cheese.
8. Then use a fork, combine ¼ minced peppers, ¼ teaspoon salt, milk, and the rest of the ingredients.
9. Pour over the bread and top with the rest of the Asiago cheese. Chill for 8 hours or overnight, covered.

3.15 Cheese and Tomato Tartlets

Cooking Time: 1 hour 10 minutes
Serving Size: 6

Ingredients:
Tomato Ragu
- 400g tomatoes
- Pinch of salt and pepper
- 1 teaspoon oregano
- 1 teaspoon sugar
- 1 tablespoon olive oil
- 2 cloves garlic
- 1 tablespoon tomato puree

- 1 onion

Tart Cases

- 320g pack pastry

Béchamel Sauce

- 85g mozzarella cheese
- ½ teaspoon black pepper
- 240ml milk
- 75g mature cheddar cheese
- 4 tablespoon plain flour
- 45g unsalted butter

Other Toppings

- 3 tablespoon cheddar cheese
- Small bunch of fresh thyme
- 12 small tomatoes
- 3 tablespoon panko breadcrumbs
- 1 small egg

Method:

1. In a moderate deep fryer or stove pan, add the oil and insert the onions.
2. Cook for five minutes over moderate flame.
3. Cook for another minute after adding the garlic.
4. Combine the tomato sauce, marjoram, sugar, canned tomatoes, salt, and pepper in a large mixing bowl.
5. Make six squares out of the puff pastry.
6. Take the beans from the stove and set them aside.
7. In a small saucepan, melt the butter.
8. Toss in the flour and mix with a fork. Slowly drizzle in the milk.
9. Combine the cheddar, prosciutto, and black pepper in a mixing bowl.
10. Fill the pastry cases with the tomatoes ragu.

3.16 Mediterranean Barbecued Lamb

Cooking Time: 18 minutes
Serving Size: 6
Ingredients:
For the Lamb
- 1 large lemon, juice of
- 1 small yellow or red onion
- Olive oil
- 2 racks of lamb
- 1 teaspoon black pepper
- 1 tablespoon mint leaves
- 1 teaspoon garlic paste
- ¼ teaspoon sweet paprika
- ½ teaspoon salt
- ½ teaspoon green cardamom
- ½ teaspoon ground nutmeg
- 1 teaspoon allspice

For the Tomato Mint Quinoa
- ½ cup red onion
- ⅓ cup feta cheese
- Salt and pepper
- 1 cup fresh mint leaves
- 3 garlic cloves
- 1 14.5 oz. can petit tomato
- Water
- 2 tablespoon olive oil
- 1 cup dry quinoa

Method:
1. Mix the garlic, seasoning, tablespoon clean, fresh mint, and two tablespoons olive oil in a shallow bowl.
2. Pick the pork chops and brush them with the paprika rub on both ends.

3. In the meantime, prepare the quinoa as per the product directions.
4. 2 tablespoon olive oil, heated in a nonstick medium saucepan.
5. Continue cooking and add diced tomato from a can. Season to taste.
6. Preheat the grill to high heat, then add the pork chops and cook for 2 minutes.
7. Heat for another three minutes on the other hand.
8. Allow ten minutes for the chops to rest while serving.

3.17 Mediterranean Lentils with Roasted Eggplant

Cooking Time: 1 hour 15 minutes
Serving Size: 4
Ingredients:
- ½ cup Greek yogurt
- Fresh ground pepper
- ¾ teaspoon fine sea salt
- 3 tablespoon fresh parsley
- 4 lbs. globe eggplants
- ½ teaspoon dried oregano
- ¼ teaspoon red pepper flakes
- 2½ tablespoon fresh lemon juice
- 3 plump cloves of garlic
- 1 bay leaf
- 2 tablespoon olive oil
- 765g water
- 20 oz. cherry tomatoes
- 175g French lentils

Method:
1. Preheat the oven to 475 degrees Fahrenheit.

2. Prick each eggplant approximately seven times all around with the tines of a knife.
3. Position the tomatoes on the bottom oven and bake until they are lightly seared and burst.
4. Transfer the lentils to a large sauté pan while the eggplants are frying.
5. Pour in the liquid and season with a pinch of salt and a diced tomato.
6. Cut the eggplants wide and pick out the pulp once they've cooled enough to treat.
7. Transfer the olive oil, ginger, lime juice, marjoram, pepper flakes, white pepper, and tarragon to the lentils and vegetables in the cup.

3.18 Green Beans Mediterranean Style

Cooking Time: 20 minutes
Serving Size: 6

Ingredients:
- 3 tablespoons olive oil
- 2 packages haricots verts
- 2 teaspoons Dijon mustard
- ½ teaspoon sugar
- 1 large shallot
- 2 tablespoons red wine vinegar
- ⅓ cup Kalamata olives

Method:
1. In a big mixing bowl, combine the first five ingredients.
2. Allow for a 10-minute rest period.
3. Insert the olive oil and season with salt and pepper to taste.

4. Green beans should be cooked for approximately 3 minutes in lightly salted water, or until vibrant and buttery; drain.
5. To stop the cooking time, submerge the beans in ice cubes; rinse and dry thoroughly.
6. Toss the beans with the olive mixture.
7. Serve at ambient temperature or cool for up to two hours.

3.19 Chicken Shawarma Fries

Cooking Time: 50 minutes
Serving Size: 6
Ingredients:
- 1- ½ lbs. russet potatoes
- Hot sauce
- 3 cloves garlic
- 1 lb. chicken breasts
- Juice of ½ lemon
- Pinch cayenne pepper
- Salt
- ¼ cup olive oil
- ½ teaspoon allspice
- Pinch cinnamon
- 1 teaspoon paprika
- ½ teaspoon turmeric
- 1 teaspoon cumin

For the Mediterranean Salsa
- Salt and pepper
- Juice of ½ - 1 lemon
- ¼ cup packed parsley
- ¼ teaspoon oregano
- 2 vine-ripened tomatoes
- ¼ small red onion
- 1 clove garlic

- 1 small cucumber

For the Garlic Sauce
- 3 cloves garlic
- Salt
- 2 tablespoons lemon juice
- ½ cup mayonnaise

Method:
1. In a big Ziploc container, mix the lime juice, 2 tablespoons of additional olive oil, herbs, and crushed garlic cloves.
2. Potatoes can be sliced into chips.
3. Preheat the oven to 400 degrees Fahrenheit, then cover a sheet pan with foil and lightly rub with nonstick cooking spray.
4. Cook the meat for 12-15 minutes after spreading it out on a cookie dish.
5. Boost the temperature to 425 degrees Fahrenheit.
6. Sprinkle the leftover two tablespoons extra virgin sunflower oil over the potatoes and sprinkle thoroughly with salt and black pepper.
7. In a blender or food processor, combine all of the Garlic Sauce components and heat until fully smooth.

3.20 Mediterranean Salmon En Papillote with Potatoes

Cooking Time: 1 hour
Serving Size: 4

Ingredients:
- 1 courgette
- 400g waxy potatoes
- 1 bag of capers
- 1 Romano pepper

- 1 lemon
- 125g cherry tomatoes
- 2 x 110g salmon fillets
- 1 bag of pitted black olives

Method:

1. Preheat the oven to 200 degrees Celsius.
2. Break the corvettes into tiny parts that are easy to eat.
3. Remove the seeds from the Romano pepper.
4. In the center of two parts, place the sliced courgette, Romano peppers, grape tomatoes, and green olives.
5. Cook the fish with a pinch of salt and place it skin-side up over the veggies.
6. Preheat the oven to 250°F and bake the tray for 25-30 minutes, or until the fish is done.
7. Drain and transfer the vegetables to the pot once they've finished cooking.
8. Offer the en papillote Mediterranean fish with the dressing potatoes on the bottom.

Chapter 4: Traditional Greek Dishes

4.1 Greek Chicken and Potatoes Recipe

Cooking Time: 1 hour
Serving Size: 4

Ingredients:
- ⅔ cup chicken broth
- Chopped oregano for garnish
- 6 cloves garlic, minced
- 3 russet potatoes
- ½ cup fresh lemon juice
- ½ cup olive oil
- 1 teaspoon rosemary
- 1 pinch cayenne pepper
- 4 pounds chicken thighs
- 1 tablespoon dried oregano
- 1 teaspoon black pepper
- 1 tablespoon kosher salt

Method:
1. Preheat the oven to 425 degrees Fahrenheit.
2. In a big mixing bowl, combine the chicken bits.
3. Add salt, oregano, cinnamon, rosemary, and smoked paprika to taste.
4. Combine the new lemon juice, olive oil, and garlic in a mixing bowl.
5. Place the chicken parts in the roasting pan that has been prepared.
6. Pour the rest of the marinade over the chicken and potatoes.
7. Preheat the oven to 350°F. Cook for 20 minutes in an oven and bake.
8. Preheat the oven to broil or the maximum temperature setting.

9. Strain the juices and pour them over the chicken and potatoes.

4.2 Mediterranean Quinoa Salad

Cooking Time: 25 minutes
Serving Size: 4
Ingredients:
- 1/3 cup fresh basil
- ¼ cup crumbled feta cheese
- ½ cup Kalamata olives
- ¼ cup sundried tomatoes
- 2 cups quinoa
- 1 cup chickpeas
- ½ small red onion
- ½ cucumber
- 1 red bell pepper

Lemon Oregano Dressing
- ¼ teaspoon ground cumin
- Salt & pepper to taste
- ½ teaspoon dried oregano
- ½ teaspoon garlic powder
- 2 tablespoon lemon juice
- 1 tablespoon Dijon mustard
- 1 teaspoon maple syrup
- 1/3 cup olive oil
- 1 tablespoon white wine vinegar

Method:
1. To make the salad, add all of the components to a big mixing bowl.
2. In a small pan, combine all of the salad dressing components.
3. Cover with the cap and move until it is well combined.

4. Taste half of the salad dressing and sprinkle it over the quinoa salad.

4.3 Mediterranean Orzo Salad

Cooking Time: 1 hour 35 minutes
Serving Size: 12
Ingredients:
- 1 clove garlic
- Kosher salt and black pepper
- 1 lemon
- 1/3 cup extra-virgin olive oil

Salad
- 1 red onion
- Kosher salt and black pepper
- 1½ cups feta cheese
- 3 tablespoons fresh parsley
- 1½ cups cherry tomatoes
- 1½ cups Kalamata olives
- 15-ounce can chickpeas
- 1½ cups grape tomatoes
- 12 ounces orzo pasta

Method:
1. Place the olive oil, lime juice, cloves, and a pinch of salt and pepper in a container or bowl until fully mixed.
2. Heat the orzo as per the package instructions in a pot of boiling water.
3. In a food processor or blender, combine the orzo, chickpeas, yellow and red tomatoes, artichokes, feta, tarragon, and vegetables.
4. Pour the seasoning over the edge.
5. Taste and season with salt and pepper if necessary.

4.4 Mediterranean-Style Greek Pasta

Cooking Time: 25 minutes
Serving Size: 4

Ingredients:

- ¼ teaspoon black pepper
- ½ cup feta cheese
- 1 beefsteak tomato large
- ½ teaspoon kosher salt
- 2 cups spinach leaves fresh
- 3 garlic cloves sliced
- 2 tablespoons olive oil
- 1 onion small
- ½ pound spaghetti pasta

Method:

1. In a small saucepan, carry 4 cups of water on the stove.
2. In a big pot of water, add 1 teaspoon of salt and the spaghetti.
3. Boil, exposed, for ten minutes or until pasta is soft.
4. Drain the pasta and set aside half a cup of the cooking water.
5. Add the oil to a large frying pan until it is hot but not burning.
6. Toss the garlic and onions into the skillet.
7. Toss in the spinach and sliced tomatoes.
8. Stir in the spinach, cover, cook over medium heat, or cook until it is cooked through and just beginning to wilt.
9. In a large mixing bowl, combine the pasta and the pasta water that has been set aside.
10. Cover and continue to cook for another five minutes.

4.5 Mediterranean One-Dish Meal

Cooking Time: 25 minutes
Serving Size: 4

Ingredients:
- 3 cups spinach
- ½ cup feta cheese
- 1 teaspoon dried oregano
- ½ cup quinoa
- ¾ pound Italian turkey sausage
- 1 can diced tomatoes
- ¼ cup Greek olives
- 2 garlic cloves
- 1 medium onion

Method:
1. Heat sausage and onions in a wide nonstick frying pan sprayed with the baking dish over moderate flame until sausage is golden brown and onions become tender.
2. Cook for an additional minute after adding the garlic.
3. Bring to a boil with the onions, olives, and marjoram.
4. Add the quinoa and mix well.
5. Reduce the heat to low, cover, and cook for 12-15 minutes, or until the liquid has been consumed.

4.6 Mediterranean Greek Power Bowls

Cooking Time: 25 minutes

Ingredients:

For the Bowls

- ¾ cup crumbled feta
- Fresh dill, for garnish
- 1 avocado
- ½ cup halved Kalamata olives
- 1 tablespoon olive oil
- 1 cup cherry tomatoes
- ½ cucumber
- Freshly ground black pepper
- 2 cup rice
- 1 teaspoon oregano
- Kosher salt
- 2 chicken breasts

For the Dressing

- Freshly ground black pepper
- ¼ cup olive oil
- 1 teaspoon dried oregano
- Kosher salt
- Juice of ½ lemon
- 2 tablespoon red wine vinegar

Method:

1. Add the oil to a large frying pan.
2. Dress with oregano, salt, and peppers before adding the chicken.
3. Cook for ten minutes per hand or until translucent and no pinker.
4. Toss tomatoes, cauliflower, diced chicken, tomato, black olives, feta, and dill into a dish of cooked quinoa or basmati rice.
5. Merge wine vinegar, lime juice, and smoked paprika in a small bowl and season to taste with salt and black pepper.

6. Slowly drizzle in the olive oil, constantly whisking to mix.

4.7 Greek Meze Platter

Cooking Time: 30 minutes
Serving Size: 6
Ingredients:
- Fresh tomatoes
- Warmed pita bread
- Feta cheese
- Baby cucumbers
- 1 cup hummus
- Dolmades
- 1 cup Tzatziki
- Greek meatballs
- Kalamata olives

Method:
1. To makes serving simpler, arrange all of the components on a wide platter in sections.
2. Drizzle vegetable oil over the cheddar cheese and season with dried oregano.
3. Drizzle some olive oil on top of the hummus and sprinkle some toasted pine nuts on top.
4. Serve with warmed flatbread.

4.8 Mediterranean Greek Yogurt Marinade

Cooking Time: 22 minutes
Serving Size: 8
Ingredients:
Dill Greek Yogurt Sauce

- Pinch cayenne pepper
- Salt, if needed
- 1 tablespoon olive oil
- Juice of ½ lemon or lime
- 1 cup fresh dill
- 1 ¼ cup Greek yogurt
- 1 garlic clove

For the Grilled Chicken

- 1 medium-size red onion
- Juice of 1-2 lemons
- 5 tablespoon olive oil
- 8 chicken thighs
- ¼ teaspoon cardamom
- Salt and pepper
- 10 garlic cloves
- ½ teaspoon allspice
- ½ teaspoon ground nutmeg
- ½ teaspoon paprika

Method:

1. Create the dill Greek yogurt sauce first.
2. In a mixing bowl, mix the chopped garlic, red pepper, yogurt, olive oil, lime juice, and smoked paprika.
3. Process the ingredients in the mixing bowl.
4. Combine the minced garlic, herbs, and three tablespoons of olive oil in a small cup.
5. Position the flavored chicken thighs in a wide dish with the leftover two tablespoon canola oil, lime juice, and diced red onions.
6. Preheat the grill for the chicken breasts.
7. Cover and barbecue for 5-6 minutes, then flip the chicken and wrap for the next 5-6 minutes.

4.9 Mediterranean One Pot Pasta

Cooking Time: 20 minutes
Serving Size: 8
Ingredients:
- ½ cup fresh dill
- ½ cup crumbled feta
- 1-pint grape tomatoes
- 1 (15 oz.) can artichoke hearts
- 16 oz. linguine
- ½ cup green olives
- ½ cup black olives
- 1 small red onion
- Four cloves garlic
- 6 cups vegetable broth

Method:
1. Combine the linguine, broth, cabbage, olives, onions, black olives, and garlic in a large mixing bowl with a few large pinches of salt and black pepper. To mix, stir all together.
2. Increase the heat to high and carry to a simmer.
3. Cook, exposed, for 10-12 minutes over moderately low heat, or till spaghetti is al dente and that most of the fluid has been consumed.
4. New dill and feta cheese are added last.
5. The feta will start to melt and combine with the residual pasta water, forming a light sauce that will coat the noodles.
6. Serve with chili flakes and a little more feta on top.

4.10 Mediterranean Meatballs with Tzatziki

Cooking Time: 25 minutes
Serving Size: 8
Ingredients:

- 2 eggs
- ½ cup panko
- 1 teaspoon cinnamon
- ½ cup flat-leaf parsley
- 2 teaspoon cumin
- 2 teaspoon oregano
- 2 lbs. ground beef
- 1 teaspoon ground pepper
- 2 teaspoon salt
- 6 garlic cloves
- 1 onion, grated

Tzatziki Sauce
- ½ teaspoon sea salt
- ¼ teaspoon black pepper
- 1-2 cloves garlic
- 1 lemon, juiced
- 1 cup Greek yogurt
- 1 tablespoon dried dill
- 2 teaspoon za'atar
- 1 small cucumber

Method:
1. Preheat the oven to 400 degrees Fahrenheit.
2. Then use a slow cooker or by hand, grate the onion.
3. Combine the ground beef, cabbage, cloves, peppers, salt, cilantro, oregano, spice, whites, pancetta, and tarragon in a stick blender or by hand until thoroughly combined.
4. Place the meatballs on two rimmed cookie sheets lined with parchment paper and lightly greased.
5. Preheat the oven to 200°F and bake for 20–25 minutes, turning the pans midway through.
6. Create the tzatziki sauce in the meantime. In a small mixing bowl, add all of the components.

7. To allow flavors to meld, protect and refrigerate for 1 hour.

Conclusion

Fresh grains, meats, vegetables, and olives are used in Mediterranean foods. Many people all over the world can follow Mediterranean dishes because of the numerous nutritional benefits they provide. The Mediterranean diet is heart-healthy because it emphasizes new, low-fat foods with no lipid. This means you should try this recipe whether you're trying to lose weight or don't like to eat unhealthy foods. While this diet includes some animal protein, the amounts are small, and it is low in fat, which is beneficial to your health. Mediterranean food is popular all over the world due to its delectable flavors and health benefits. This diet has the advantage of allowing you to consume clean, nutritious foods. Since the diet is mainly fruits, nuts, and veggies, you are also mindful of what you are consuming. Try Mediterranean recipes and make healthier meals for your family.

PESCATARIAN

COOKBOOK

70 Recipes for Preparing at Home Healthy Fish and Seafood Dishes.

Maki Blanc

The trademarks that are used are without any consent, and the publication of the trademark is without permission or backing by the trademark owner. All trademarks and brands within this book are for clarifying purposes only and are owned by the owners themselves, not affiliated with this document.

Introduction

People are bringing more variety into their eating routines, and many want to add fish into their eating plans as eating certain fish species can add protein and hold fat admission down. A Pescatarian diet is an eating regimen that bars meat and poultry yet incorporates plant food varieties, fishes, dairy and eggs. Pescatarians can eat any fish and devour food from plants, dairy and eggs sources.

Pescatarians are vegetarians who fill their essential protein source with the help of seafood in their diet. The Pescatarian diet improves your diet and lifestyle habits. However, you will be eating undeniably a larger number of vegetables than meat, and vegetables will, in general, have fewer calories and less fat. In this way, you will have an eating routine normally lower in calories and fat admission.

This book promotes healthy eating and contains 70 different recipes that you can easily follow with the detailed ingredient list and easy-to-understand instructions list below each recipe. The recipe list contains breakfast, lunch, dinner, and snack recipes.

Chapter 1: The World of Pescatarian Breakfast Recipes

The basic thing more regrettable than a terrible breakfast is having nothing at all to eat in the morning. Fortunately, that will not be an issue for you. We have assembled a setup of the absolute best pescatarian breakfast recipes you would love to make yourself. Following are the recipes listed below:

1.1 Salmon Muffins Recipe

Preparation Time: 20 minutes

Cooking Time: 20 minutes

Serving: 4

Ingredients:

- Dried thyme, half teaspoon
- Smoked salmon, one and a half cup
- Large eggs, ten
- Garlic powder, half teaspoon
- Grated cheddar cheese, one cup
- Mozzarella cheese, one cup
- Chopped fresh dill, one cup
- Salt, to taste
- Black pepper, to taste

- Onion powder, one teaspoon
- Chopped cilantro, a quarter cup

Instructions:

1. Take a large bowl.
2. Add the eggs into the bowl.
3. Add the chopped dill into the bowl of eggs.
4. Add the garlic powder and onion powder into the bowl.
5. Add the cheddar and mozzarella cheese into the eggs.
6. Mix the eggs until all the mixture is uniformly mixed.
7. Add the dried thyme, smoked salmon meat, salt and pepper.
8. Add the egg mixture into the muffin tray.
9. Bake the muffins for about ten to fifteen minutes.
10. Add the chopped cilantro on top.
11. Your dish is ready to be served.

1.2 Shrimp and Scallion Pancakes Recipe

Preparation Time: 30 minutes

Cooking Time: 15 minutes

Serving: 4

Ingredients:

- Ground garlic, half teaspoon
- Salt, as required
- Shrimp, one cup
- Ground pepper, as required
- Scallions, one cup
- Cilantro as required
- Coconut oil, two tablespoon
- Tapioca flour, half cup
- Almond flour, half cup
- Coconut milk, one cup
- Ground ginger, half teaspoon

Instructions:

1. Mix in both the flours in a bowl.
2. Add the chopped or sliced scallions.
3. Add in the spices, deboned shrimps and cilantro.

4. Mix the ingredients carefully.

5. Add the mixture in small quantities in a pan.

6. Let the pancakes turn golden on both sides.

7. Add a little cilantro on top of the pancakes.

8. You can garnish the pancakes with any other thing that you prefer.

9. Your dish is ready to be served.

1.3 Avocado and Crab Toast Recipe

Preparation Time: 30 minutes

Cooking Time: 15 minutes

Serving: 4

Ingredients:

- Olive oil, two tablespoon
- Garlic powder, one tablespoon
- Salt to taste
- Pepper to taste
- Paprika, one tablespoon
- Onion diced, one cup
- Parsley, one tablespoon
- Crab meat, one cup
- Tomatoes, one cup
- Cheese slices, as required

- Bread slices, as required
- Avocado slices, one cup
- Yeast, two teaspoon

Instructions:
1. Take a pan and add the olive oil into it.
2. Heat the oil well.
3. Add parsley, garlic powder, paprika and tomatoes.
4. Cook them for five minutes.
5. Then you can add onions.
6. Cook the mixture again and keep stirring.
7. Add pieces of crab meat.
8. Continue to cook the ingredients for few minutes.
9. Lay the mixture onto a slice of bread.
10. Add the avocado slices on top of the meat.
11. Add a cheese slice on top and cover it with another bread slice.
12. Cook the bread slices on both sides.
13. You can serve it with any dip of your choice.
14. Your dish is ready to serve.

1.4 Smoked Salmon Toast Recipe

Preparation Time: 30 minutes

Cooking Time: 15 minutes

Serving: 4

Ingredients:

- Olive oil, two tablespoon
- Garlic powder, one tablespoon
- Salt to taste
- Pepper to taste
- Paprika, one tablespoon
- Onion diced, one cup
- Parsley, one tablespoon
- Smoked salmon, one cup
- Tomatoes, one cup
- Cheese slices, as required
- Bread slices, as required
- Yeast, two teaspoon

Instructions:

1. Take a pan and add the olive oil into it.
2. Heat the oil well.
3. Add parsley, garlic powder, paprika and tomatoes.
4. Cook them for five minutes.
5. Then you can add onions.
6. Cook the mixture again and keep stirring.
7. Add pieces of smoked salmon.
8. Continue to cook the ingredients for few minutes.

9. Lay the mixture onto a slice of bread.

10. Add a cheese slice on top and cover it with another bread slice.

11. Cook the bread slices on both sides.

12. You can serve it with any dip of your choice.

13. Your dish is ready to serve.

1.5 Shrimp and Guacamole Quesadillas Recipe

Preparation Time: 10 minutes

Cooking Time: 20 minutes

Serving: 2

Ingredients:

- Olive oil, two cups
- Garlic powder, one tablespoon
- Salt to taste
- Pepper to taste
- Paprika, one tablespoon
- Onion diced, one cup
- Parsley, one tablespoon
- Shrimp meat, one cup
- Tomatoes, one cup
- Guacamole paste, one cup

- Cheese slices, as required
- Tortilla sheets, four

Instructions:

1. Take a pan and add olive oil into it.
2. Heat the oil well.
3. Add parsley, garlic powder, paprika and tomatoes.
4. Cook them for five minutes.
5. Then you can add onions.
6. Cook the mixture again and keep stirring.
7. Add pieces of deboned shrimps.
8. Continue to cook the ingredients for few minutes.
9. Lay the mixture onto a tortilla sheet.
10. Add the guacamole mixture on top of the meat.
11. Add a cheese slice on top and cover it with another tortilla.
12. Cook the tortilla sheets on both sides.
13. You can serve it with any sauce of your choice.
14. Your dish is ready to be served.

1.6 Avocado and Tuna Salad Recipe

Preparation Time: 10 minutes

Cooking Time: 30 minutes

Serving: 2

Ingredients:

- Tuna pieces, half pound
- Maple syrup, one teaspoon
- Ground ginger, a quarter teaspoon
- Avocados, two
- Pecan pieces, two tablespoon
- Pepper, as required
- Cilantro, half cup
- Salt, a quarter teaspoon
- Greek yoghurt, as required
- Greek salad dressing, half cup

Instructions:

1. Peel the avocados and then cut them into large pieces.
2. Boil the tuna pieces, drain them and slice them into a bowl.

3. Mix all the ingredients along with the avocados and tuna.

4. In a bowl, add the salad dressing and beat it well.

5. Drizzle the dressing on top of the avocados and tuna mixture.

6. Your dish is ready to be served.

1.7 Salmon Burgers Recipe

Preparation Time: 20 minutes

Cooking Time: 20 minutes

Serving: 4

Ingredients:

- Burger buns, as required
- Minced salmon meat, one cup
- Bread crumbs, one cup
- Egg, one
- Chopped parsley, half cup
- Fresh chopped cilantro, half cup
- Salt, to taste
- Black pepper, to taste
- Olive oil, for frying
- Greek yoghurt, half cup
- Lemon juice, a quarter cup

- Fresh chopped dill, two tablespoon
- Butter, one tablespoon

Instructions:

1. Take a large bowl.
2. Add the salmon meat, salt, pepper, bread crumbs and egg into it.
3. Mix all the ingredients well.
4. Add the chopped cilantro and parsley into the mixture.
5. Mix the ingredients until they become smooth.
6. Shape the mixture into patties.
7. In a large pan, add the olive oil and cook the patties.
8. Cook the patties until they turn golden brown from both sides.
9. Meanwhile, in a small bowl, add the Greek yoghurt, lemon juice, and fresh dill.
10. Mix it to form a paste.
11. Add butter to your buns and heat them.
12. Add the salmon patty to the bread slice.
13. Add the paste on top of the patty and cover it with the burger bun.
14. The salmon burger is ready to be served.

1.8 Greek Salmon Burritos Recipe

Preparation Time: 10 minutes

Cooking Time: 20 minutes

Serving: 2

Ingredients:

- Olive oil, two cups
- Garlic powder, one tablespoon
- Salt to taste
- Pepper to taste
- Paprika, one tablespoon
- Onion diced, one cup
- Parsley, one tablespoon
- Salmon meat, one cup
- Tomatoes, one cup
- Jalapeno slices, as required
- Greek yoghurt, one cup
- Avocado slices, as required
- Tortilla sheets, four

Instructions:

1. Add the olive oil into a pan.
2. Heat the oil well.

3. Add the onions.

4. Cook the onions well until they turn soft.

5. Add parsley, garlic powder, paprika and tomatoes.

6. Cook them for five minutes.

7. Cook the mixture again and keep stirring.

8. Add pieces of salmon meat.

9. Continue to cook the ingredients for few minutes.

10.   Lay the mixture onto a tortilla sheet.

11.   Add the Greek yoghurt on top of the meat.

12.   Add the rest of the ingredients on top and roll it into a burrito.

13.   Heat the burrito.

14.   You can serve it with any sauce of your choice.

15.   Your dish is ready to be served.

1.9 Tomato, Asparagus and Tuna Muffins Recipe

Preparation Time: 20 minutes

Cooking Time: 20 minutes

Serving: 4

Ingredients:

- Chopped tomatoes, one cup
- Chopped asparagus, one cup
- Dried thyme, half teaspoon
- Tuna meat, one and a half cup
- Large eggs, ten
- Garlic powder, half teaspoon
- Grated cheddar cheese, one cup
- Mozzarella cheese, one cup
- Chopped fresh dill, one cup
- Salt, to taste
- Black pepper, to taste
- Onion powder, one teaspoon
- Chopped cilantro, a quarter cup

Instructions:

1. Take a large bowl.

2. Beat the eggs into the bowl.

3. Add the chopped dill into the bowl of eggs.

4. Add the garlic powder and onion powder into the bowl.

5. Add the cheddar and mozzarella cheese into the eggs.

6. Mix the eggs until all the mixture is uniformly mixed.

7. Add the dried thyme, chopped tomatoes, chopped asparagus and tuna meat, salt and pepper.

8. Add the egg mixture into the muffin tray.

9. Bake the muffins for about ten to fifteen minutes.

10. Add the chopped cilantro on top.

11. Your dish is ready to be served.

1.10 Salmon Scrambled Eggs Recipe

Preparation Time: 25 minutes

Cooking Time: 15 minutes

Serving: 4

Ingredients:

- Chopped garlic, two teaspoon
- Green onions, three tablespoon
- Tomato, half cup
- Salmon, two cups

- Chopped fresh dill, two tablespoon
- Vegetable oil, two tablespoon
- Soy sauce, two tablespoon
- Salt to taste
- Black pepper to taste
- Chopped fresh cilantro, one tablespoon
- Eggs, eight
- Chopped onions, two tablespoon

Instructions:

1. Heat a pan.
2. Add the oil into the pan.
3. Add the garlic and onions.
4. Add the salmon and cook on medium-high warmth for several seconds or until they begin to take on a changed tone.
5. Add in the tomato cook until delicate, however, to some degree crispy.
6. Turn down the warmth and pour the beaten eggs and leave to set for a couple of moments.
7. Scramble egg mixture.
8. Add in the soy sauce and chopped dill.
9. Add some salt and pepper.
10. Garnish it with chopped cilantro leaves.
11. Your dish is ready to be served.

1.11 Boiled Eggs and Sardine Salad Recipe

Preparation Time: 10 minutes

Cooking Time: 30 minutes

Serving: 2

Ingredients:

- Sardine pieces, half pound
- Lemon juice, one teaspoon
- Ground ginger, a quarter teaspoon
- Avocados, two
- Chopped almonds, two tablespoon
- Pepper, as required
- Cilantro, half cup
- Eggs, two
- Salt, a quarter teaspoon
- Greek yoghurt, as required
- Salad dressing, half cup

Instructions:

1. Boil the eggs, peel them, and then cut them into large pieces.
2. Boil the sardine pieces, drain them, and slice them into a bowl.

3. Mix all the ingredients along with the sardines and eggs.

4. In a bowl, add the salad dressing and beat it well.

5. Drizzle the dressing on top of the sardine and egg mixture.

6. The salad is ready to be served.

1.12 Tuna and Avocado Burgers Recipe

Preparation Time: 20 minutes

Cooking Time: 20 minutes

Serving: 4

Ingredients:

- Burger buns, as required
- Minced tuna meat, one cup
- Bread crumbs, one cup
- Avocado slices, as required
- Egg, one
- Chopped parsley, half cup
- Fresh chopped cilantro, half cup
- Salt, to taste
- Black pepper, to taste
- Olive oil, for frying
- Greek yoghurt, half cup
- Lemon juice, a quarter cup
- Fresh chopped dill, two tablespoon
- Butter, one tablespoon

Instructions:

1. Take a large bowl.

2. Add the tuna meat, salt, pepper, bread crumbs, and egg into it.

3. Mix all the ingredients well.

4. Add the chopped cilantro and parsley into the mixture.

5. Mix the ingredients until they become smooth.

6. Shape the mixture into patties.

7. In a large pan, add the olive oil and cook the patties.

8. Cook the patties until they turn golden brown from both sides.

9. Meanwhile, in a small bowl, add the Greek yoghurt, lemon juice and fresh dill.

10. Mix it to form a paste.

11. Add butter to your buns and heat them.

12. Add the tuna patty to the bread slice.

13. Add the paste on top of the patty.

14. Add the avocado slices on top of the paste and cover it with the burger bun.

15. The tuna and the avocado burger are ready to be served.

Chapter 2: The World of Pescatarian Lunch Recipes

Following are some classic pescatarian lunch recipes that are rich in healthy nutrients, and you can easily make them with the detailed instructions list in each recipe:

2.1 Buttery Grilled Shrimp Recipe

Preparation Time: 10 minutes

Cooking Time: 25 minutes

Serving: 2

Ingredients:

- Powdered cumin, one tablespoon
- Salt, to taste
- Black pepper, to taste
- Turmeric powder, one teaspoon
- Onion, one cup
- Vegetable broth, one cup
- Smoked paprika, half teaspoon
- Unboned shrimp pieces, one pound
- Minced garlic, two tablespoon
- Minced ginger, two tablespoon

- Cilantro, half cup
- Butter, two tablespoon
- Chopped tomatoes, one cup
- Grated ginger, two tablespoon

Instructions:

1. Take a pan.
2. Add the oil and onions into the pan.
3. Cook the onions until they become soft and fragrant.
4. Add in the chopped garlic and ginger.
5. Cook the mixture and add the tomatoes into it.
6. Add the spices and shrimps.
7. Mix the shrimps so that the tomatoes and spices are coated all over the shrimps.
8. Grill the shrimps for fifteen minutes.
9. When the shrimps are done, add in the cilantro.
10. The dish is ready to be served.

2.2 Fajita Styled Shrimp and Grits Recipe

Preparation Time: 30 minutes

Cooking Time: 20 minutes

Serving: 4

Ingredients:

- Shrimp pieces, three cup
- Fajita spice powder, one teaspoon
- Cooking grits, one cup
- Smoked paprika, half teaspoon
- Shredded Mexican cheese blend, half cup
- Minced garlic, two tablespoon
- Minced ginger, two tablespoon
- Orange juice, half cup
- Olive oil, two tablespoon
- Chopped tomatoes, one cup
- Bell peppers, two cups
- Salsa, one cup
- Water, four cups

Instructions:

1. Boil the water in a large saucepan.
2. Add the cooking grits into it.
3. Cook grits until the mixture turns thick.
4. Add the olive oil into a large pan.
5. Add the garlic, ginger, shrimps and fajita spice powder into the pan.
6. Cook shrimps and then add the bell peppers.
7. Add all the spices and tomatoes into the mixture.
8. Cook the mixture for five minutes and then add the orange juice into the mixture.
9. Dish out shrimp and bell peppers when they are done.
10. Add a spoon full of grits and salsa on top.
11. Your dish is ready to be served.

2.3 Pretzel Crusted Catfish Recipe

Preparation Time: 10 minutes

Cooking Time: 30 minutes

Serving: 2

Ingredients:

- Catfish, one pound
- Orange juice, one tablespoon
- Garlic powder, one tablespoon
- Chili powder, half tablespoon

- Olive oil, one cup
- Cilantro, one tablespoon
- Mayonnaise, one cup
- Avocado, two slices
- Salt to taste
- Pepper to taste
- Cooking oil, as required
- Crushed pretzels, one cup

Instructions:

1. Wash the catfish and let it dry.
2. Take a small bowl.
3. Add orange juice, garlic powder and mayonnaise into the bowl.
4. Add chili powder and pepper.
5. Then add cilantro and mix them all well.
6. Add all the ingredients together to form a smooth paste.
7. Add the catfish into the mixture and coat well.
8. Coat each catfish piece in the crusted pretzels and then deep fry the fish.
9. Dish out fish when it turns golden brown.
10. Your dish is ready to be served.

2.4 Garlic and Herb Salmon Sliders Recipe

Preparation Time: 20 minutes

Cooking Time: 20 minutes

Serving: 4

Ingredients:

- Burger buns, as required
- Minced salmon meat, one cup
- Bread crumbs, one cup
- Egg, one
- Fresh Italian herbs, half cup
- Fresh chopped cilantro, half cup
- Salt, to taste
- Black pepper, to taste
- Olive oil, for frying
- Lemon juice, a quarter cup
- Fresh chopped garlic, two tablespoon
- Butter, one tablespoon

Instructions:

1. Take a large bowl.
2. Add the salmon meat, chopped garlic, lemon juice, salt, pepper, bread crumbs and egg into it.

3. Mix all the ingredients well.

4. Add the chopped cilantro and fresh Italian herbs into the mixture.

5. Mix the ingredients until they become smooth.

6. Shape the mixture into patties.

7. In a large pan, add the olive oil and cook the patties.

8. Cook the patties until they turn golden brown from both sides.

9. Add butter on your buns and heat them.

10. Add the salmon patty on the bread slice.

11. Cover the patty with the burger bun.

12. The salmon sliders are ready to be served.

2.5 Feta and Tomato Basil Fish Recipe

Preparation Time: 10 minutes

Cooking Time: 40 minutes

Serving: 2

Ingredients:

- Fresh basil leaves, one cup
- Mix spice, one teaspoon
- Onion, one cup
- Salmon pieces, half pound
- Smoked paprika, half teaspoon

- Chopped cilantro, as required
- Minced garlic, two tablespoon
- Minced ginger, two tablespoon
- Lemon juice, half cup
- Butter, two tablespoon
- Chopped cilantro, as required
- Fresh herbs, one tablespoon
- Chopped tomatoes, one cup
- Feta cheese, one cup

Instructions:

1. Take a large pan.
2. Add in the butter and onions.
3. Cook the onions until they become soft and fragrant.
4. Add in the chopped garlic and ginger.
5. Cook the mixture and add the tomatoes into it.
6. Add the spices and feta cheese.
7. When the tomatoes are done, add the salmon pieces into it.
8. Mix the ingredients carefully and cover the pan.
9. Add in the remaining ingredients in the end and cook it for five minutes.
10. Dish out when salmon is done.
11. Garnish it with chopped fresh cilantro.
12. Your dish is ready to be served.

2.6 Grilled Pistachio and Lemon Pesto Shrimp Recipe

Preparation Time: 10 minutes

Cooking Time: 25 minutes

Serving: 2

Ingredients:

- Lemon juice, half cup
- Salt, to taste
- Black pepper, to taste
- Lemon zest, one teaspoon
- Onion, one cup
- Vegetable broth, one cup
- Smoked paprika, half teaspoon
- Unboned shrimp pieces, one pound
- Minced garlic, two tablespoon
- Minced ginger, two tablespoon
- Cilantro, half cup
- Butter, two tablespoon
- Pesto paste, one cup
- Crushed pistachio, half cup
- Grated ginger, two tablespoon

Instructions:

1. Take a large bowl.
2. Add in the chopped garlic and ginger.
3. Mix the mixture and add the pesto paste into it.
4. Add the spices and shrimps.
5. Add the rest of the ingredients into the bowl.
6. Mix the shrimps so that all the spices are coated all over the shrimps.
7. Grill the shrimps for fifteen minutes with butter.
8. Dish out the shrimps and add the cilantro on top.
9. The dish is ready to be served.

2.7 Spicy Shrimp Curry Recipe

Preparation Time: 10 minutes

Cooking Time: 40 minutes

Serving: 2

Ingredients:

- Red chili paste, two tablespoon
- Vegetable broth, one cup
- Turmeric powder, one teaspoon
- Onion, one cup
- Boneless shrimps, two cups

- Smoked paprika, half teaspoon
- Water, one cup
- Mixed vegetables, two cups
- Mix spices, two tablespoon
- Minced garlic, two tablespoon
- Minced ginger, two tablespoon
- Cilantro, half cup
- Olive oil, two tablespoon
- Chopped tomatoes, one cup

Instructions:

1. Take a pan.
2. Add the oil and onions into the pan.
3. Cook the onions until they become soft and fragrant.
4. Add in the chopped garlic and ginger.
5. Cook the mixture and add the tomatoes into it.
6. Add the spices.
7. When the tomatoes are done, add the spices into it.
8. Add in the broth, shrimps and vegetables.
9. Mix the ingredients carefully and cover your pan.
10. Cook the ingredients for fifteen to twenty minutes.
11. Add cilantro on top.
12. Your dish is ready to be served.

2.8 Chiplote and Lime Shrimp Bake Recipe

Preparation Time: 10 minutes

Cooking Time: 25 minutes

Serving: 2

Ingredients:

- Chiplote sauce, one cup
- Powdered cumin, one tablespoon
- Salt, to taste
- Black pepper, to taste
- Turmeric powder, one teaspoon
- Onion, one cup
- Lemon juice, half cup
- Vegetable broth, one cup
- Smoked paprika, half teaspoon
- Shrimp pieces, one pound
- Minced garlic, two tablespoon
- Minced ginger, two tablespoon
- Cilantro, half cup
- Olive oil, two tablespoon
- Chopped tomatoes, one cup
- Grated ginger, two tablespoon

Instructions:

1. Take a pan.

2. Add in the oil and onions.

3. Cook the onions until they become soft and fragrant.

4. Add in the chopped garlic and ginger.

5. Cook the mixture and add the tomatoes into it.

6. Add the spices, lemon juice, chiplote sauce, and shrimp.

7. Mix the shrimp so that the tomatoes and spices are coated all over the shrimp.

8. Bake the shrimp for fifteen minutes.

9. Dish out the shrimp once they are done.

10.   Garnish it with chopped cilantro.

11.   Your dish is ready to be served.

2.9 Lemon Shrimp with Parmesan Rice Recipe

Preparation Time: 10 minutes

Cooking Time: 25 minutes

Serving: 2

Ingredients:

- Parmesan cheese, one cup

- Powdered cumin, one tablespoon
- Salt, to taste
- Black pepper, to taste
- Turmeric powder, one teaspoon
- Onion, one cup
- Lemon juice, half cup
- Vegetable broth, one cup
- Smoked paprika, half teaspoon
- Shrimp pieces, one pound
- Minced garlic, two tablespoon
- Minced ginger, two tablespoon
- Cilantro, half cup
- Olive oil, two tablespoon
- Cooked rice, one cup
- Grated ginger, two tablespoon

Instructions:
1. Take a pan.
2. Add in the oil and onions.
3. Cook the onions until they become soft and fragrant.
4. Add in the chopped garlic and ginger.
5. Cook the mixture and add the tomatoes into it.
6. Add the spices, lemon juice and shrimps.

7. Mix the shrimps so that the tomatoes and spices are coated all over the shrimps.

8. Cook the cod for fifteen minutes.

9. Add the cooked rice and parmesan cheese into the mixture.

10. Your dish is ready to be served.

2.10 Tuna Steak on Fettuccine Recipe

Preparation Time: 10 minutes

Cooking Time: 25 minutes

Serving: 2

Ingredients:

- Fish broth, one cup
- Turmeric powder, one teaspoon
- Onion, one cup
- Tuna pieces, one cup
- Smoked paprika, half teaspoon
- Salt and black pepper, to taste
- Minced garlic, two tablespoon
- Minced ginger, two tablespoon
- Cilantro, half cup
- Olive oil, two tablespoon
- Fettucine pasta, one pack

Instructions:

1. Take a pan.
2. Add the oil and onions into the pan.
3. Cook the onions until they become soft and fragrant.
4. Add in the chopped garlic and ginger.
5. Cook the mixture well.
6. Add the spices.
7. Add in the broth.
8. Add the tuna pieces.
9. Cook the tuna on both sides.
10. Boil fettuccine according to the instructions on the package.
11. Drain fettuccine and add it into a plate.
12. Dish out tuna pieces when the tuna pieces are done.
13. Place the tuna pieces on the fettucine.
14. Add cilantro on top.
15. Your dish is ready to be served.

2.11 Cajun Shrimp Skillet Recipe

Preparation Time: 30 minutes

Cooking Time: 20 minutes

Serving: 4

Ingredients:

- Dried thyme, half teaspoon
- Powdered ginger, half teaspoon
- Powdered garlic, half teaspoon
- Cherry tomatoes, two cups
- Cajun spice, two tablespoon
- Sea salt, to taste
- Olive oil, two tablespoon
- Onion, one
- Shrimps, one pound
- Lemon juice, one cup

Instructions:

1. Heat the olive oil in a skillet
2. Add in the powdered spices.
3. Add all the ingredients along with the shrimps.
4. Cook the mixture for five to ten minutes or until the shrimps are cooked.
5. Mix it well and cook for five additional minutes.
6. Your dish is ready to be served.

2.12 Cajun Seafood Grill Recipe

Preparation Time: 10 minutes

Cooking Time: 25 minutes

Serving: 2

Ingredients:

- Lemon juice, half cup
- Salt, to taste
- Black pepper, to taste
- Lemon zest, one teaspoon
- Onion, one cup
- Vegetable broth, one cup
- Smoked paprika, half teaspoon
- Seafood, one pound
- Minced garlic, two tablespoon
- Minced ginger, two tablespoon
- Cilantro, half cup
- Butter, two tablespoon
- Cajun seasoning, half cup
- Grated ginger, two tablespoon

Instructions:

1. Take a large bowl.

2. Add in the chopped garlic and ginger.

3. Mix the mixture and add the Cajun spice into it.

4. Add the spices and seafood.

5. Add the rest of the ingredients into the bowl.

6. Mix the seafood so that all the spices are coated all over the seafood.

7. Grill the seafood for fifteen minutes with butter.

8. Dish out the seafood shrimps and add the cilantro on top.

9. The dish is ready to be served.

2.13 Grilled Lobster Tails Recipe

Preparation Time: 10 minutes

Cooking Time: 25 minutes

Serving: 2

Ingredients:

- Lemon juice, half cup
- Salt, to taste
- Black pepper, to taste
- Lemon zest, one teaspoon
- Onion, one cup
- Vegetable broth, one cup
- Smoked paprika, half teaspoon
- Lobster tails, one pound

- Minced garlic, two tablespoon
- Minced ginger, two tablespoon
- Cilantro, half cup
- Olive oil, two tablespoon
- Tomato paste, one cup
- Grated ginger, two tablespoon

Instructions:
1. Take a large bowl.
2. Add in the chopped garlic and ginger.
3. Mix the mixture and add the tomato paste into it.
4. Add the spices and lobsters.
5. Add the rest of the ingredients into the bowl.
6. Mix the lobsters so that all the spices are coated all over the lobsters.
7. Grill the lobsters for fifteen minutes with olive oil.
8. Dish out the lobsters and add the cilantro on top.
9. The dish is ready to be served.

2.14 Scallops in Sage Cream Recipe

Preparation Time: 10 minutes
Cooking Time: 40 minutes
Serving: 2

Ingredients:

- Full cream, one cup
- Mix spice, one teaspoon
- Onion, one cup
- Scallops pieces, half pound
- Smoked paprika, half teaspoon
- Chopped cilantro, as required
- Minced garlic, two tablespoon
- Minced ginger, two tablespoon
- Lemon juice, half cup
- Butter, two tablespoon
- Chopped cilantro, as required
- Fresh herbs, one tablespoon
- Chopped tomatoes, one cup
- Chopped sage, one cup

Instructions:
1. Take a large pan.
2. Add in the butter and onions.
3. Cook the onions until they become soft and fragrant.
4. Add in the chopped garlic and ginger.
5. Cook the mixture and add the tomatoes into it.
6. Add the spices and full cream.

7. When the tomatoes are done, add the scallop pieces into it.

8. Mix the ingredients carefully and cover your pan.

9. Add in the remaining ingredients in the end and cook it for five minutes.

10. Dish out when your scallops are done.

11. Garnish it with chopped fresh cilantro.

12. Your dish is ready to be served.

2.15 Shrimp Alfredo Pasta Recipe

Preparation Time: 10 minutes

Cooking Time: 25 minutes

Serving: 2

Ingredients:

- Full cream, one cup
- Italian herbs, one teaspoon
- Onion, one cup
- Shrimp pieces, one cup
- Smoked paprika, half teaspoon
- Water, one cup
- Minced garlic, two tablespoon
- Minced ginger, two tablespoon
- Cilantro, half cup

- Olive oil, two tablespoon
- Pasta, one pack

Instructions:

1. Take a pan.
2. Add the oil and onions into it.
3. Cook the onions until they become soft and fragrant.
4. Add in the chopped garlic and ginger.
5. Cook the mixture and add the shrimps into it.
6. Add the spices.
7. Add in the full cream.
8. Mix the ingredients carefully and cover your pan.
9. Boil the pasta according to the instructions on the package.
10. Drain the pasta.
11. Mix the pasta into the mixture.
12. Add cilantro on top.
13. Your dish is ready to be served.

2.16 Brown Butter Salmon with Tomatoes Recipe

Preparation Time: 10 minutes

Cooking Time: 25 minutes

Serving: 2

Ingredients:

- Powdered cumin, one tablespoon
- Salt, to taste
- Black pepper, to taste
- Turmeric powder, one teaspoon
- Onion, one cup
- Vegetable broth, one cup
- Smoked paprika, half teaspoon
- Salmon pieces, one pound
- Minced garlic, two tablespoon
- Minced ginger, two tablespoon
- Cilantro, half cup
- Butter, two tablespoon
- Cherry tomatoes, one cup
- Grated ginger, two tablespoon

Instructions:

1. Take a pan.
2. Add the oil and onions into the pan.
3. Cook the onions until they become soft and fragrant.
4. Add in the chopped garlic and ginger.
5. Cook the mixture and add the tomatoes into it.
6. Add the spices and salmon pieces.
7. Mix the salmon pieces so that the spices are coated all over the salmon pieces.
8. Cook the salmon for fifteen minutes.
9. Dish out salmon and tomatoes.
10. Garnish it with chopped cilantro.
11. The dish is ready to be served.

2.17 Salmon Avocado Salad Recipe

Preparation Time: 10 minutes

Cooking Time: 30 minutes

Serving: 2

Ingredients:

- Smoked salmon pieces, half pound
- Lemon juice, one teaspoon
- Ground ginger, a quarter teaspoon
- Avocados, two
- Chopped almonds, two tablespoon

- Pepper, as required
- Cilantro, half cup
- Salt, a quarter teaspoon
- Greek yoghurt, as required
- Salad dressing, half cup

Instructions:

1. Mix all the ingredients along with the salmon and avocados.
2. In a bowl, add the salad dressing and beat it well.
3. Drizzle the dressing on top of the salmon and avocados mixture.
4. The salad is ready to be served.

2.18 Shrimp Pasta with Lemon and Spinach Recipe

Preparation Time: 10 minutes

Cooking Time: 25 minutes

Serving: 2

Ingredients:

- Lemon juice, half cup
- Chopped spinach, two cups

- Full cream, one cup
- Italian herbs, one teaspoon
- Onion, one cup
- Shrimp pieces, one cup
- Smoked paprika, half teaspoon
- Water, one cup
- Minced garlic, two tablespoon
- Minced ginger, two tablespoon
- Cilantro, half cup
- Olive oil, two tablespoon
- Pasta, one pack

Instructions:

1. Take a pan.
2. Add the oil and onions into it.
3. Cook the onions until they become soft and fragrant.
4. Add in the chopped garlic and ginger.
5. Cook the mixture and add the shrimps into it.
6. Add the spices and lemon juice.
7. Add in the chopped spinach.
8. Mix the ingredients carefully and cover your pan.
9. Boil the pasta according to the instructions on the package.
10. Drain the pasta.

11.   Mix the pasta and full cream into the mixture.

12.   Add cilantro on top.

13.   Your dish is ready to be served.

2.19 Pan Seared Fish Recipe

Preparation Time: 10 minutes

Cooking Time: 25 minutes

Serving: 2

Ingredients:

- Powdered cumin, one tablespoon
- Salt, to taste
- Black pepper, to taste
- Turmeric powder, one teaspoon
- Onion, one cup
- Smoked paprika, half teaspoon
- Fish filet pieces, one pound
- Minced garlic, two tablespoon
- Minced ginger, two tablespoon
- Cilantro, half cup
- Olive oil, two tablespoon

Instructions:

1. Take a large bowl.

2. Add the oil and onions into the bowl.

3. Add the chopped garlic and ginger into the bowl.

4. Add the spices.

5. Add the cilantro into it.

6. Mix all the ingredients.

7. Add the fish pieces with the mixture into a pan.

8. Cook fish pieces.

9. Dish them out when cooked properly.

10.   Sprinkle some cilantro on top.

11.   Your dish is ready to be served.

2.20 Grilled Harissa Shrimp with Ginger Sauce Recipe

Preparation Time: 10 minutes

Cooking Time: 25 minutes

Serving: 2

Ingredients:

- Harissa, half cup
- Salt, to taste
- Black pepper, to taste
- Lemon zest, one teaspoon
- Onion, one cup
- Vegetable broth, one cup

- Smoked paprika, half teaspoon
- Shrimp pieces, one pound
- Minced garlic, two tablespoon
- Minced ginger, two tablespoon
- Cilantro, half cup
- Olive oil, two tablespoon
- Tomato paste, one cup
- Ginger sauce, half cup

Instructions:

1. Take a large bowl.
2. Add in the chopped garlic.
3. Mix the mixture and add the tomato paste into it.
4. Add the spices and shrimps.
5. Add the rest of the ingredients into the bowl.
6. Mix the shrimps so that all the spices are coated all over the shrimps.
7. Grill the shrimps for fifteen minutes with olive oil.
8. Dish out the shrimps and add the cilantro on top.
9. The dish is ready to be served.

2.21 Salmon Skewers Recipe

Preparation Time: 10 minutes

Cooking Time: 25 minutes

Serving: 2

Ingredients:

- Lemon juice, one tablespoon
- Salt, to taste
- Black pepper, to taste
- Mix spice, one teaspoon
- Onion, one cup
- Smoked paprika, half teaspoon
- Salmon filet pieces, one pound
- Minced garlic, two tablespoon
- Minced ginger, two tablespoon
- Cilantro, half cup
- Olive oil, two tablespoon
- Wooden skewers, as required

Instructions:

1. Take a large bowl.
2. Add the oil and onions into the bowl.
3. Add the chopped garlic and ginger into the bowl.

4. Add the spices.

5. Add the cilantro into it.

6. Mix all the ingredients together.

7. Add the salmon pieces with the mixture into the wooden skewers.

8. Cook your skewers.

9. Dish them out when cooked properly.

10. Sprinkle some cilantro on top.

11. Your dish is ready to be served.

2.22 Mango Curry Shrimp Recipe

Preparation Time: 10 minutes

Cooking Time: 40 minutes

Serving: 2

Ingredients:

- Vegetable broth, one cup
- Turmeric powder, one teaspoon
- Onion, one cup
- Boneless shrimps, two cups
- Smoked paprika, half teaspoon
- Water, one cup
- Mango pieces, two cups
- Mix spices, two tablespoon
- Minced garlic, two tablespoon

- Minced ginger, two tablespoon
- Cilantro, half cup
- Olive oil, two tablespoon
- Chopped tomatoes, one cup

Instructions:

1. Take a pan.
2. Add the oil and onions into the pan.
3. Cook the onions until they become soft and fragrant.
4. Add in the chopped garlic and ginger.
5. Cook the mixture and add the tomatoes into it.
6. Add the spices.
7. When the tomatoes are done, add the spices into it.
8. Add in the broth, shrimps and mangoes.
9. Mix the ingredients carefully and cover your pan.
10. Cook the ingredients for fifteen to twenty minutes.
11. Add cilantro on top.
12. Your dish is ready to be served.

2.23 Baked Almond Crusted Cod Recipe

Preparation Time: 10 minutes

Cooking Time: 25 minutes

Serving: 2

Ingredients:

- Powdered cumin, one tablespoon
- Salt, to taste
- Black pepper, to taste
- Turmeric powder, one teaspoon
- Onion, one cup
- Smoked paprika, half teaspoon
- Dijon mustard, half cup
- Cod pieces, one pound
- Minced garlic, two tablespoon
- Minced ginger, two tablespoon
- Cilantro, half cup
- Olive oil, two tablespoon
- Almond flour, three tablespoon
- Sliced almond, half cup

Instructions:
1. Take a large bowl.
2. Add the oil and onions into the bowl.
3. Add the chopped garlic and ginger into the bowl.
4. Add the tomatoes into the bowl.
5. Add the spices.
6. Add the cilantro into it.
7. Mix all the ingredients together.

8. Add the almond flour and mix ingredients.

9. Cover codpieces with the mixture above.

10.   Bake codpieces.

11.   Dish them out when cooked properly.

12.   Sprinkle some cilantro and sliced almond on top.

13.   You can serve it with any of your preferred sauces.

14.   Your dish is ready to be served.

Chapter 3: The World of Pescatarian Dinner Recipes

Following are some classic pescatarian dinner recipes that are rich in healthy nutrients and you can easily make them with the detailed instructions list in each recipe:

3.1 Stir Fried Shrimp and Mushrooms Recipe

Preparation Time: 30 minutes

Cooking Time: 10 minutes

Serving: 4

Ingredients:

- Vegetable broth, one cup
- Turmeric powder, one teaspoon
- Onion, one cup
- Mushrooms, two cups
- Smoked paprika, half teaspoon
- Water, one cup
- Shrimps, two cups
- Mixed spices, two tablespoon
- Minced garlic, two tablespoon
- Minced ginger, two tablespoon

- Cilantro, half cup
- Olive oil, two tablespoon
- Chopped tomatoes, one cup

Instructions:
1. Take a pan.
2. Add in the oil and onions.
3. Cook the onions until they become soft and fragrant.
4. Add in the chopped garlic and ginger.
5. Cook the mixture and add the tomatoes into it.
6. Add the spices and sauces.
7. When the tomatoes are done, add the shrimps and mushrooms into it.
8. Cook for five minutes.
9. When cooked, dish it out.
10. Garnish it with chopped cilantro leaves
11. Your dish is ready to be served.

3.2 Basil and Lemon Crab Linguini Recipe

Preparation Time: 10 minutes

Cooking Time: 25 minutes

Serving: 2

Ingredients:

- Lemon juice, half cup
- Chopped basil, two cups
- Full cream, one cup
- Italian herbs, one teaspoon
- Onion, one cup
- Crabmeat, one cup
- Smoked paprika, half teaspoon
- Water, one cup
- Minced garlic, two tablespoon
- Minced ginger, two tablespoon
- Cilantro, half cup
- Olive oil, two tablespoon
- Linguini, one pack

Instructions:

1. Take a pan.
2. Add the oil and onions into it.
3. Cook the onions until they become soft and fragrant.
4. Add in the chopped garlic and ginger.
5. Cook the mixture and add the crab meat into it.
6. Add the spices and lemon juice.
7. Add in the chopped basil.
8. Mix the ingredients carefully and cover your pan.
9. Boil the linguini according to the instructions on the package.
10. Drain the linguini.
11. Mix the linguini and full cream into the mixture.
12. Add cilantro on top.
13. Your dish is ready to be served.

3.3 Crab Topped Fish Fillets Recipe

Preparation Time: 25 minutes

Cooking Time: 15 minutes

Serving: 4

Ingredients:

- Chopped garlic, two teaspoon

- Green onions, three tablespoon
- Bread crumbs, half cup
- Crabmeat, two cups
- Fish filets, one pound
- Chopped fresh dill, two tablespoon
- Vegetable oil, two tablespoon
- Salt to taste
- Black pepper to taste
- Eggs, two
- Chopped onions, two tablespoon

Instructions:

1. In a large bowl, add in the onions and the garlic.
2. Add in the rest of the ingredients.
3. In a pan, heat the vegetable oil.
4. Fry the fish filets.
5. Dish out filets when they turn golden brown on both sides.
6. Your dish is ready to be served.

3.4 Pesto and Shrimp Pasta Recipe

Preparation Time: 10 minutes

Cooking Time: 25 minutes

Serving: 2

Ingredients:

- Pesto paste, half cup
- Full cream, one cup
- Italian herbs, one teaspoon
- Onion, one cup
- Shrimp pieces, one cup
- Smoked paprika, half teaspoon
- Water, one cup
- Minced garlic, two tablespoon
- Minced ginger, two tablespoon
- Cilantro, half cup
- Olive oil, two tablespoon
- Pasta, one pack

Instructions:
1. Take a pan.
2. Add the oil and onions into it.

3. Cook the onions until they become soft and fragrant.

4. Add in the chopped garlic and ginger.

5. Cook the mixture and add the shrimps into it.

6. Add the spices and pesto paste.

7. Mix the ingredients carefully and cover pan.

8. Boil the pasta according to the instructions on the package.

9. Drain the pasta.

10.   Mix the pasta and full cream into the mixture.

11.   Add cilantro on top.

12.   Your dish is ready to be served.

3.5 Shrimp Stew Recipe

Preparation Time: 10 minutes

Cooking Time: 40 minutes

Serving: 2

Ingredients:

- Fish broth, one cup
- Turmeric powder, one teaspoon
- Onion, one cup
- Lemon juice, half cup
- Shrimp mince, half pound

- Powdered cumin, half tablespoon
- Smoked paprika, half teaspoon
- Water, one cup
- Minced garlic, two tablespoon
- Minced ginger, two tablespoon
- Cilantro, half cup
- Olive oil, two tablespoon
- Chopped tomatoes, one cup

Instructions:

1. Take a pan.
2. Add in the oil and onions.
3. Cook the onions until they become soft and fragrant.
4. Add in the chopped garlic and ginger.
5. Cook the mixture and add the tomatoes into it.
6. Add the spices and shrimp mince.
7. Add in the broth.
8. Mix the ingredients carefully and cover your pan.
9. Add cilantro on top.
10. Your dish is ready to be served.

3.6 Seared Scallops with Citrus and Herb Sauce Recipe

Preparation Time: 10 minutes

Cooking Time: 25 minutes

Serving: 2

Ingredients:

- Orange juice, one cup
- Powdered cumin, one tablespoon
- Salt, to taste
- Black pepper, to taste
- Turmeric powder, one teaspoon
- Onion, one cup
- Smoked paprika, half teaspoon
- Scallop pieces, one pound
- Minced garlic, two tablespoon
- Minced ginger, two tablespoon
- Cilantro, half cup
- Heavy cream, half cup
- Italian herbs, two tablespoon
- Olive oil, two tablespoon

Instructions:

1. Take a large bowl.

2. Add the oil and onions into the bowl.

3. Add the chopped garlic and ginger into the bowl.

4. Add the spices.

5. Add the cilantro into it.

6. Mix all the ingredients together.

7. Add the scallop pieces with the mixture into a pan.

8. Add the orange juice, herbs and heavy cream into the pan.

9. Dish them out when cooked properly.

10.   Garnish with some cilantro on top.

11.   Your dish is ready to be served.

3.7 Shrimp Puttanesca Recipe

Preparation Time: 10 minutes

Cooking Time: 25 minutes

Serving: 2

Ingredients:

- White wine, half cup
- Cherry tomatoes, one cup
- Italian herbs, one teaspoon
- Onion, one cup
- Green olives, half cup
- Shrimp pieces, one cup
- Smoked paprika, half teaspoon
- Water, one cup
- Minced garlic, two tablespoon
- Minced ginger, two tablespoon
- Cilantro, half cup
- Olive oil, two tablespoon
- Spaghetti, one pack

Instructions:

1. Take a pan.
2. Add the oil and onions into it.
3. Cook the onions until they become soft and fragrant.
4. Add in the chopped garlic and ginger.
5. Cook the mixture and add the shrimps into it.
6. Add the spices and cherry tomatoes.
7. Mix the ingredients carefully and cover your pan.
8. Boil the spaghetti according to the instructions on the package.
9. Drain the spaghetti.
10. Mix the spaghetti and white wine into the mixture.
11. Add green olives and cilantro on top.
12. Your dish is ready to be served.

3.8 Salmon and Spud Salad Recipe

Preparation Time: 10 minutes

Cooking Time: 30 minutes

Serving: 2

Ingredients:

- Smoked salmon pieces, half pound

- Lemon juice, one teaspoon
- Ground ginger, a quarter teaspoon
- Chopped cooked spuds, two
- Chopped almonds, two tablespoon
- Pepper, as required
- Cilantro, half cup
- Salt, a quarter teaspoon
- Greek yoghurt, as required
- Salad dressing, half cup

Instructions:

1. Mix all the ingredients along with the salmon and spuds.
2. In a bowl, add the salad dressing and beat it well.
3. Drizzle the dressing on top of the salmon and spuds mixture.
4. The salad is ready to be served.

3.9 Tomato Poached Halibut Recipe

Preparation Time: 10 minutes

Cooking Time: 30 minutes

Serving: 2

Ingredients:

- Halibut pieces, half pound
- Ground ginger, a quarter teaspoon
- Pecan pieces, two tablespoon
- Tomato paste, one cup
- Pepper, as required
- Red chili powder, one teaspoon
- Cilantro, half cup
- Salt, a quarter teaspoon
- Red chili paste, one tablespoon
- Greek yoghurt, as required
- Peanuts, half cup

Instructions:

1. Boil the halibut pieces.
2. In a large pan, add all the ingredients except the halibut pieces.
3. Cook your tomato sauce.
4. Add the halibut pieces and let them simmer for five to ten minutes.
5. Add peanuts and Greek yoghurt on top.
6. Your dish is ready to be served.

3.10 Cilantro and Lime Shrimp Recipe

Preparation Time: 10 minutes

Cooking Time: 40 minutes

Serving: 2

Ingredients:

- Onion, one cup
- Shrimp pieces, half pound
- Smoked paprika, half teaspoon
- Chopped cilantro, as required
- Minced garlic, two tablespoon
- Minced ginger, two tablespoon
- Lemon juice, half cup
- Butter, two tablespoon
- Fresh herbs, one tablespoon
- Chopped tomatoes, one cup

Instructions:

1. Take a large pan.
2. Add in the butter and onions.
3. Cook the onions until they become soft and fragrant.
4. Add in the chopped garlic and ginger.
5. Cook the mixture and add the tomatoes into it.
6. Add the salt, pepper, and fresh herbs.
7. When the tomatoes are done, add the shrimp pieces into it.

8. Mix the ingredients carefully and cover your pan.

9. When done, dish it out.

10. Add fresh chopped cilantro on top.

11. Your dish is ready to be served.

3.11 Citrus Scallops Recipe

Preparation Time: 10 minutes

Cooking Time: 25 minutes

Serving: 2

Ingredients:

- Orange juice, one cup
- Powdered cumin, one tablespoon
- Salt, to taste
- Black pepper, to taste
- Turmeric powder, one teaspoon
- Onion, one cup
- Smoked paprika, half teaspoon
- Scallop pieces, one pound
- Minced garlic, two tablespoon
- Minced ginger, two tablespoon
- Cilantro, half cup
- Lemon juice, half cup
- Olive oil, two tablespoon

Instructions:

1. Take a large bowl.
2. Add the oil and onions into the bowl.
3. Add the chopped garlic and ginger into the bowl.
4. Add the spices.
5. Add the cilantro into it.
6. Mix all the ingredients together.
7. Add the scallop pieces with the mixture into a pan.
8. Add the orange juice, and lemon juice into the pan.
9. Dish them out when cooked properly.
10. Garnish with some cilantro on top.
11. Your dish is ready to be served.

3.12 Rosemary and Garlic Shrimp Recipe

Preparation Time: 30 minutes

Cooking Time: 10 minutes

Serving: 4

Ingredients:

- Vegetable broth, one cup
- Turmeric powder, one teaspoon
- Onion, one cup

- Rosemary herbs, half cup
- Smoked paprika, half teaspoon
- Water, one cup
- Shrimps, two cups
- Mixed spices, two tablespoon
- Minced garlic, two tablespoon
- Cilantro, half cup
- Olive oil, two tablespoon
- Chopped tomatoes, one cup

Instructions:

1. Take a pan.
2. Add in the oil and onions.
3. Cook the onions until they become soft and fragrant.
4. Add in the chopped garlic.
5. Cook the mixture and add the tomatoes into it.
6. Add the spices and sauces.
7. When the tomatoes are done, add the shrimps and rosemary herbs into it.
8. Cook for five minutes.
9. When cooked, dish it out.
10. Garnish it with chopped cilantro leaves
11. Your dish is ready to be served.

3.13 Spicy Mango Scallops Recipe

Preparation Time: 10 minutes

Cooking Time: 40 minutes

Serving: 2

Ingredients:

- Red chili paste, two tablespoon
- Turmeric powder, one teaspoon
- Onion, one cup
- Scallops, two cups
- Smoked paprika, half teaspoon
- Water, one cup
- Mango pieces, two cups
- Mix spices, two tablespoon
- Minced garlic, two tablespoon
- Minced ginger, two tablespoon
- Cilantro, half cup
- Olive oil, two tablespoon
- Chopped tomatoes, one cup

Instructions:

1. Take a pan.
2. Add the oil and onions into the pan.

3. Cook the onions until they become soft and fragrant.

4. Add in the chopped garlic and ginger.

5. Cook the mixture and add the tomatoes into it.

6. Add the spices.

7. When the tomatoes are done, add the spices into it.

8. Add in the red chili paste, scallops and mangoes.

9. Mix the ingredients carefully and cover your pan.

10. Cook the ingredients for fifteen to twenty minutes.

11. Add cilantro on top.

12. Your dish is ready to be served.

3.14 Cornmeal Catfish with Avocado Sauce Recipe

Preparation Time: 10 minutes

Cooking Time: 30 minutes

Serving: 2

Ingredients:

- Catfish, one pound
- Orange juice, one tablespoon
- Garlic powder, one teaspoon
- Lemon juice, half cup

- Chili powder, half tablespoon
- Olive oil, one cup
- Cilantro, one tablespoon
- Salt to taste
- Pepper to taste
- Cooking oil, as required
- Crushed cornmeal, one cup
- Avocado sauce, as required

Instructions:

1. Wash the catfish and let it dry.
2. Take a small bowl.
3. Add orange juice, garlic powder and lemon juice into the bowl.
4. Add chili powder and pepper.
5. Then add cilantro and mix them all well.
6. Add all the ingredients together to form a smooth paste.
7. Add the catfish into the mixture and coat well.
8. Coat each catfish piece in the crusted cornmeal, and then deep fry the fish.
9. Dish out your fish when it turns golden brown.
10. Drizzle the avocado sauce on top of the catfish.
11. Your dish is ready to be served.

3.15 Lime Boiled Catfish Recipe

Preparation Time: 10 minutes

Cooking Time: 30 minutes

Serving: 2

Ingredients:

- Catfish, one pound
- Orange juice, one tablespoon
- Garlic powder, one teaspoon
- Chili powder, half tablespoon
- Olive oil, one cup
- Cilantro, one tablespoon
- Salt to taste
- Pepper to taste
- Cooking oil, as required
- Lime juice, one cup
- Lime zest, one tablespoon

Instructions:

1. Wash the catfish and let it dry.
2. Take a small bowl.

3. Add orange juice, garlic powder, lime zest and lime juice into the bowl.

4. Add chili powder and pepper.

5. Then add cilantro and mix them all well.

6. Add all the ingredients together to form a smooth paste.

7. Add the catfish into the mixture and coat well.

8. Steam the fish.

9. Dish out the fish when it cooks properly.

10. You can serve it with any sauce.

11. Your dish is ready to be served.

3.16 Southwestern Catfish Recipe

Preparation Time: 10 minutes

Cooking Time: 25 minutes

Serving: 2

Ingredients:

- Mix spice, one tablespoon
- Salt, to taste
- Black pepper, to taste
- Turmeric powder, one teaspoon
- Onion, one cup
- Smoked paprika, half teaspoon
- Catfish pieces, one pound

- Minced garlic, two tablespoon
- Minced ginger, two tablespoon
- Cilantro, half cup
- Olive oil, two tablespoon
- Chopped tomatoes, one cup
- Grated ginger, two tablespoon

Instructions:

1. Take a pan.
2. Add the oil and onions into the pan.
3. Cook the onions until they become soft and fragrant.
4. Add in the chopped garlic and ginger.
5. Cook the mixture and add the tomatoes into it.
6. Add the spices and catfish.
7. Mix the catfish so that the tomatoes and spices are coated all over the catfish.
8. Grill the shrimps for fifteen minutes.
9. Garnish with chopped cilantro.
10. The dish is ready to be served.

3.17 Breaded Sea Scallops Recipe

Preparation Time: 10 minutes

Cooking Time: 30 minutes

Serving: 2

Ingredients:

- Garlic powder, one cup
- Chili powder, half tablespoon
- Olive oil, one cup
- Scallops, one pound
- Cilantro, one tablespoon
- Mayonnaise, one cup
- Bread crumbs, two cups
- Salt to taste
- Pepper to taste

Instructions:

1. Wash the scallops and let it dry.
2. Take a small bowl.
3. Add the scallops into it.
4. Add all the spices.
5. Add salt and pepper as required.
6. Then add cilantro and mix them all well.
7. Marinate the scallops for an hour.
8. After marinating, coat the fish in the bread crumbs.
9. Fry it until the scallops turn golden brown.
10. Your dish is ready to be served.

3.18 Deep Fried Catfish Recipe

Preparation Time: 10 minutes

Cooking Time: 30 minutes

Serving: 2

Ingredients:

- Catfish, one pound
- Orange juice, one tablespoon
- Garlic powder, one teaspoon
- Lemon juice, half cup
- Chili powder, half tablespoon
- Olive oil, one cup
- Cilantro, one tablespoon
- Chopped parsley, as required
- Salt to taste
- Pepper to taste
- Cooking oil, as required

Instructions:

1. Wash the catfish and let it dry.
2. Take a small bowl.

3. Add orange juice, garlic powder and lemon juice into the bowl.

4. Add chili powder and pepper.

5. Then add cilantro and mix them all well.

6. Add all the ingredients together to form a smooth paste.

7. Add the catfish into the mixture and coat well.

8. Deep fry the catfish.

9. Dish out your fish when it turns golden brown.

10. Add fresh chopped parsley on top.

11. Your dish is ready to be served.

3.19 One Pot Roasted Halibut Recipe

Preparation Time: 10 minutes

Cooking Time: 30 minutes

Serving: 2

Ingredients:

- Turmeric powder, one teaspoon
- Onion, one cup
- Halibut filet pieces, half pound
- Smoked paprika, half teaspoon
- Minced garlic, two tablespoon
- Minced ginger, two tablespoon
- Lemon juice, half cup

- Olive oil, two tablespoon
- Chopped tomatoes, one cup

Instructions:

1. Take a pan.
2. Add in the oil and onions.
3. Cook the onions until they become soft and fragrant.
4. Add in the chopped garlic and ginger.
5. Cook the mixture and add the tomatoes into it.
6. Add the spices.
7. When the tomatoes are done, add the halibut pieces into it.
8. Mix the ingredients carefully and place your mixture into the oven.
9. Add cilantro on top.
10. Drizzle any preferred sauce on top of your fish.
11. Your dish is ready to be served.

3.20 Instant Pot Steamed Cod with Ginger Sauce Recipe

Preparation time: 10 minutes

Cooking Time: 20 minutes

Serving: 4

Ingredients:

- Cod, one pound
- Ginger sauce, half cup
- Lime juice, half cup
- Lemon juice, half cup
- Tomatoes, two
- Red onion, one cup
- Cilantro, half cup
- Salt, to taste
- Pepper, to taste

Instructions:

1. Heat an instant pot.
2. Add all the ingredients into the pot.
3. Add the cod pieces into the mixture.
4. Cover the instant pot.
5. Dish out the mixture when the cod is cooked.

6. Garnish it with chopped cilantro on top.

7. Your dish is ready to be served.

3.21 Shrimp Stuffed Avocados Recipe

Preparation time: 10 minutes
Cooking Time: 20 minutes
Serving: 4

Ingredients:

- Shrimp, one pound
- Avocados, as required
- Lime juice, half cup
- Lemon juice, half cup
- Tomatoes, two
- Red onion, one cup
- Cilantro, half cup
- Cucumber, half cup
- Salt, to taste
- Pepper, to taste

Instructions:

1. Bring a pot of water to boil.

2. Add the shrimp to boiling water and cook it in steam.

3. Drain the shrimp and add it in the ice water.

4. Take a large bowl and add the shrimp into it.

5. Add the lemon juice, lime juice and cilantro into it.

6. Add the pepper and salt in it to season it.

7. Mix them thoroughly.

8. Peel the avocados and remove the seed.

9. Add the mixture into the avocados and serve.

10. Your dish is ready to be served.

3.22 Cod and Pesto Pasta Recipe

Preparation time: 30 minutes

Cooking Time: 40 minutes

Serving: 4

Ingredients:

- Pesto pasta, one cup
- Cod, one pound
- Minced garlic, two tablespoon
- Minced ginger, two tablespoon
- Cilantro, half cup
- Sesame oil, two tablespoon
- Corn flour, two tablespoon

- Water, half cup
- Vegetable stock, two cup
- Chopped tomatoes, one cup
- Italian parsley, one cup
- Onion, one cup
- Pasta, one pack
- Oregano, one teaspoon
- Water, one cup

Instructions:

1. Take a pan.
2. Add in the oil and onions.
3. Cook the onions until they become soft and fragrant.
4. Add the cod and pesto into it.
5. Add in the chopped garlic and ginger.
6. Cook the mixture and add the tomatoes into it.
7. Add the spices, sauces and white wine.
8. When the tomatoes are done, add the pasta into it.
9. Add in the vegetable broth.
10. Mix the ingredients carefully and cover your pan.
11. Cook the mixture for twenty minutes.
12. Add cilantro on top.
13. Your dish is ready to be served.

3.23 Steamed Shrimps with Mint Recipe

Preparation Time: 10 minutes

Cooking Time: 20 minutes

Serving: 4

Ingredients:

- Shrimp, one pound
- Mint sauce, half cup
- Lime juice, half cup
- Lemon juice, half cup
- Tomatoes, two
- Red onion, one cup
- Cilantro, half cup
- Salt, to taste
- Pepper, to taste

Instructions:

1. Bring a pot of water to boil.
2. Add the shrimp to boiling water and cook it in steam.
3. Drain the shrimp and add it in the ice water.
4. Take a large bowl and add the shrimp into it.
5. Add the lemon juice, lime juice and cilantro into it.

6. Add the pepper and salt in it to season it.

7. Mix them thoroughly.

8. Steam it for ten minutes.

9. Add the mint sauce as required.

10.   Your dish is ready to be served.

Chapter 4: The World of Pescatarian Snack Recipes

Following are some yummy pescatarian snack recipes that are rich in healthy nutrients, and you can easily make them with the detailed instructions list in each recipe:

4.1 Avocado Crab Boats Recipe

Preparation time: 10 minutes

Cooking Time: 25 minutes

Serving: 4

Ingredients:

- Avocados, two
- Eggs, two
- Salt, one tablespoon
- Pepper, to taste
- Bread crumbs, one cup
- Vegetable oil, one cup
- Flour, half cup
- Water, half cup

Instructions:

1. Take a saucepan and heat it well.
2. Add the vegetable oil into it.
3. Heat the oil and cut the avocado in slices.
4. Take a bowl and add the flour into it.
5. Add the eggs, salt and pepper.
6. Mix them gently and add the avocado slices into it.
7. Then coat the avocado slices into the bread crumbs.
8. Fry it well until it becomes brown.
9. Your dish is ready to be served.

4.2 Fish and Fries Recipe

Preparation time: 10 minutes

Cooking Time: 25 minutes

Serving: 4

Ingredients:

- Flour, half cup
- Fish, one pound
- Potato, one cup
- Ginger, one tablespoon
- Garlic powder, two teaspoon
- Salt, to taste

- Pepper, to taste

Instructions:

1. Take a saucepan and heat it well.
2. Add the vegetable oil into it.
3. Heat the oil and cut the fish in pieces.
4. Take a bowl and add the flour into it.
5. Add the garlic powder and ginger in it.
6. Then add the eggs, salt and pepper.
7. Mix them gently and make a paste-type mixture.
8. Add the fish pieces into it.
9. Coat the fish pieces into bread crumbs.
10. Fry it until it becomes brown.
11. Your dish is ready to be served.

4.3 Classic Crab Cakes Recipe

Preparation time: 30 minutes

Cooking Time: 25 minutes

Serving: 4

Ingredients:

- All-purpose flour, one cup
- Crabmeat, one cup
- Baking powder, one tablespoon

- Baking soda, half tablespoon
- Egg, two
- Milk, one cup
- Vegetable oil, one cup
- Salt, half tablespoon
- Oil, one cup

Instructions:

1. Take a large bowl and add the all-purpose flour in it
2. Add the crab meat in it and mix well.
3. Add the baking powder, and salt into it.
4. Mix well until a good mixture is obtained.
5. Take another bowl and add the eggs into it.
6. Add the milk and a little oil into it.
7. Combine them well, so that a good mixture is formed.
8. Form round balls from the crab mixture and then dip it into the egg mixture.
9. Fry the balls until a light brown color comes.
10. Your dish is ready to be served.

4.4 Skinny Crab Quiche Recipe

Preparation time: 20 minutes

Cooking Time: 20 minutes

Serving: 4

Ingredients:

- Crabmeat, one cup
- Pie crust, two
- Heavy cream, one cup
- Cheese, one cup
- Green onions, one cup
- Baking soda, half tablespoon
- Egg, two
- Milk, one cup
- Vegetable oil, one cup
- Salt, half tablespoon
- Oil, one cup

Instructions:

1. Take a large bowl and add the all-purpose flour in it
2. Add the crab meat in it and mix well.
3. Add the baking powder, and salt into it.
4. Mix well until a good mixture is obtained.
5. Take another bowl and add the eggs into it.
6. Add the milk into it and a little oil into it.
7. Combine the mixture in both bowls.
8. Bake the pie crust for ten minutes.

9. Pour the above-prepared mixture into it.

10.   Bake it for twenty minutes until a light brown color comes.

11.   Your dish is ready to be served.

4.5 Asian Salmon Tacos Recipe

Preparation time: 20 minutes

Cooking Time: 20 minutes

Serving: 2

Ingredients:

- Salmon, one pound
- Green onion, half cup
- Kosher salt, one tablespoon
- Tomatoes, two
- Avocado slices, two
- Cilantro, to garnish
- Red onions, one cup
- Ginger, one tablespoon
- Garlic powder, two teaspoon
- Sesame oil, one teaspoon
- Salt, to taste
- Pepper, to taste

Instructions:

1. Take a large bowl and add salmon pieces into it.

2. Add the ginger and garlic powder to it.

3. Add the tomatoes and red onion into it.

4. Mix well until a good mixture is obtained.

5. Add the soy sauce and mix well.

6. Toss the cilantro into the sauce.

7. Add the salt and pepper as you like.

8. Cook the salmon mixture for twenty minutes.

9. Bake it until it becomes golden and slightly crisp.

10. Once the salmon is cooked, fill the tacos with it.

11. Your dish is ready to be served.

4.6 Seafood Ceviche Recipe

Preparation time: 10 minutes

Cooking Time: 20 minutes

Serving: 4

Ingredients:

- Shrimp, one pound
- Lime juice, half cup
- Lemon juice, half cup
- Tomatoes, two
- Red onion, one cup
- Cilantro, half cup

- Cucumber, half cup
- Avocado slices, one cup
- Salt, to taste
- Pepper, to taste

Instructions:

8. Bring a pot of water to boil.

9. Add the shrimp to boiling water and cook it.

10. Drain the shrimp and add it in the ice water.

11. Take a large bowl and add the shrimp into it.

12. Add the lemon juice, lime juice and cilantro into it.

13. Add the pepper and salt in it to season it.

14. Mix them thoroughly.

15. Refrigerate it for thirty minutes.

16. Add the cucumber and avocado slices on top.

17. Your dish is ready to be served.

4.7 Salmon Sticks with Hummus Recipe

Preparation time: 30 minutes

Cooking Time: 25 minutes

Serving: 4

Ingredients:

- Hummus, one cup
- Salmon fillets, four
- Arugula, two cups
- Cilantro, one
- Red bell pepper, one tablespoon
- Cheese, one cup
- Whole wheat panko, one cup
- Butter, half cup
- Honey, two tablespoon
- Lemon juice, one cup
- Garlic powder, two tablespoon
- Ginger, one tablespoon
- Soy sauce, one tablespoon
- Salt, to taste
- Sriracha, as required

Instructions:

1. Take a large bowl and add the salmon fillets into it.
2. Add the ginger and garlic powder to it.
3. Mix well until a good mixture is obtained.
4. Add the cilantro and mix gently.
5. Add the panko, cheese and honey into it.

6. Distribute the mixture evenly over the salmon fillets.

7. Add the lemon juice, olive oil and soy sauce.

8. Add the salt and pepper as you like.

9. Bake the salmon for twenty minutes

10. Serve the sticks with hummus.

11. Your dish is ready to be served.

4.8 Tuna Fritters Recipe

Preparation time: 20 minutes

Cooking Time: 10 minutes

Serving: 4

Ingredients:

- Cheese, one cup
- Tuna, three
- Bread crumbs, three
- Diced onion, one cup
- Vegetable oil, one cup
- Salt, one tablespoon
- Milk, one cup
- Black pepper, one tablespoon
- Eggs, two
- Lemon juice, one tablespoon

Instructions:

1. Take a saucepan and heat it well.
2. Add the vegetable oil into it.
3. Heat the oil and cut the fish in pieces.
4. Take a bowl and add the flour into it.
5. Add the garlic powder and ginger in it.
6. Then add the eggs, salt and pepper.
7. Add the cheese and diced onions into it.
8. Mix them gently and make a paste-type material.
9. Then add the tuna pieces into it.
10. Then coat the tuna pieces into bread crumbs.
11. Fry it well until it becomes light brown.
12. Your dish is ready to be served.

4.9 Roasted Salmon Fries Recipe

Preparation time: 15 minutes

Cooking Time: 25 minutes

Serving: 4

Ingredients:

- Flour, half cup
- Salmon Fish, one pound
- Potato, one cup
- Ginger, one tablespoon
- Garlic powder, two teaspoon
- Salt, to taste
- Pepper, to taste
- Bread crumbs, as required

Instructions:

1. Take a saucepan and heat it well.
2. Add the vegetable oil into it.
3. Heat the oil and cut the fish in pieces.
4. Take a bowl and add the flour into it.
5. Add the garlic powder and Ginger in it.
6. Then add the eggs, salt and pepper.

7. Mix them gently and make a paste-type material.

8. Then add the fish pieces into it.

9. Then coat the fish pieces into bread crumbs.

10. Fry it well until it becomes brown.

11. Your dish is ready to be served.

4.10 Fish Stuffed Mushrooms Recipe

. **Preparation time:** 20 minutes

Cooking Time: 20 minutes

Serving: 2

Ingredients:

- Fish, one pound
- Mushrooms, one pound
- Bread crumbs, as required
- Green onion, half cup
- Kosher salt, one tablespoon
- Tomatoes, two
- Avocado slices, two
- Cilantro, to garnish
- Red onions, one cup
- Ginger, one tablespoon
- Garlic powder, two teaspoon
- Sesame oil, one teaspoon
- Salt, to taste

- Pepper, to taste

Instructions:
1. Take a large bowl and add fish pieces into it.
2. Add the ginger and garlic powder to it.
3. Add the tomatoes and red onion into it.
4. Mix well until a good mixture is obtained.
5. Add the soy sauce and mix well.
6. Toss the cilantro into the sauce.
7. Add the salt and pepper as you like.
8. Cook the fish mixture for twenty minutes.
9. Once the fish is cooked, fill the mushrooms with it.
10. Bake it until it becomes golden and slightly crisp.
11. Your dish is ready to be served.

4.11 Fish Pie Fillets Recipe

Preparation time: 30 minutes

Cooking Time: 25 minutes

Serving: 4

Ingredients:

- Fish fillets, four
- Arugula, two cups

- Cilantro, one
- Red bell pepper, one tablespoon
- Cheese, one cup
- Whole wheat panko, one cup
- Butter, half cup
- Honey, two tablespoon
- Lemon juice, one cup
- Garlic powder, two tablespoon
- Ginger, one tablespoon
- Soy sauce, one tablespoon
- Salt, to taste
- Sriracha, as required

Instructions:
1. Take a large bowl and add the Fish fillets into it.
2. Add the ginger and garlic powder to it.
3. Mix well until a good mixture is obtained.
4. Add the cilantro and mix gently.
5. Add the panko, cheese and honey into it.
6. Distribute the mixture evenly over the fish fillets.
7. Add the lemon juice, olive oil and soy sauce.
8. Add the salt and pepper as you like.
9. Bake the fish for twenty minutes
10. Your dish is ready to be served.

4.12 Fish Pasta Soup Recipe

Preparation time: 30 minutes

Cooking Time: 40 minutes

Serving: 4

Ingredients:

- Pasta, two cups
- Eggs, two
- Fish, one pound
- Minced garlic, two tablespoon
- Minced ginger, two tablespoon
- Cilantro, half cup
- Sesame oil, two tablespoon
- Corn flour, two tablespoon
- Water, half cup
- Vegetable stock, two cup
- Chopped tomatoes, one cup
- Italian parsley, one cup
- Onion, one cup
- Mixed vegetables, half pound
- Oregano, one teaspoon
- Water, one cup

Instructions:

1. Take a pan.
2. Add in the oil and onions.
3. Cook the onions until they become soft and fragrant.
4. Add in the chopped garlic and ginger.
5. Cook the mixture and add the tomatoes into it.
6. Add the spices and sauces and the white wine.
7. When the tomatoes are done, add the mixed vegetables into it.
8. Add the vegetable broth and pasta into the pan.
9. Mix the ingredients carefully and cover your pan.
10. Boil the mixture for twenty minutes.
11. Mix the soup continuously for five minutes.
12. Add cilantro on top.
13. Your dish is ready to be served.

Conclusion

In the current world, we have become exceptionally aware of our wellbeing. We generally favor a natural eating regimen over other falsely developed food sources. Being on a tight eating routine has been the most well-known answer we get when we get some information about someone's wellbeing. It is a renowned saying, "your wellbeing is straightforwardly relative to your emotional health," on the off chance that you practice good eating habits and eat right, you are continually going to have inspiring and positive thinking towards life.

This cookbook incorporates 70 healthy plans that contain pescatarian breakfast, pescatarian lunch, pescatarian dinner, and pescatarian snack recipes that you can undoubtedly make at home without the help of any kind. Start cooking with this amazing and easy cookbook.

Printed in Great Britain
by Amazon

46970629R00116